I0083503

A DAUGHTER

of the most high King

KIM HERMAN

CLAY BRIDGES
PRESS

A Daughter of the Most High King

Published by Clay Bridges in Houston, TX
www.ClayBridgesPress.com

eISBN-10: 1-939815-76-2 | eISBN-13: 978-1-939815-76-7
ISBN-10: 1-939815-84-3 | ISBN-13: 978-1-939815-84-2

Special Sales: Most Clay Bridges titles are available in special quantity discounts. Custom imprinting or excerpting can also be done to fit special needs. Contact Clay Bridges at Info@ClayBridgesPublishing.com.

*This book is dedicated
to my Lord and Savior Jesus Christ.
He put this book on my heart, and in obedience to him,
I have written it.*

*It is my humble prayer that you,
my dear reader, will deepen your relationship with Jesus Christ
and that this book will cause you to walk alongside him
each and every day.*

Table of Contents

Special Thanks

My husband, Ken, who has been by my side for 30 years, has encouraged me to follow where the Lord leads me. He is an amazing husband, father, grandfather, and son of the most high King. I have been truly blessed to be his wife.

My close friend Kim Mason has been a major helper, supporter, and encourager throughout this process. We are sisters in Christ, and she has been consistent in her belief in me. Kim has gently reminded me of my goals for this book. She has patiently read through my manuscripts, editing and making thoughtful suggestions. This book would not have been possible without her.

My four sisters—Kelly, Pam, Stacie, and Sherri—have been supportive, each giving their unique talents and skills to this project. Kelly has offered advice for the business and accounting aspects of the book. Pam took the pictures of me on our family farm. Stacie has been instrumental in setting up my social media accounts. Sherri was the first of them to read a very rough draft of this book and has been a fantastic encourager.

PART ONE

Anne's Purpose

For we are God's handiwork,
created in Christ Jesus to do good works,
which God prepared in advance for us to do.

—Eph. 2:10

CHAPTER 1

The warm sun shone brightly on an early fall day. Anne enjoyed the gentle transition from summer to fall. She said a prayer of thanksgiving as she took in the beauty that surrounded her. She and Tom had purchased the small 60-acre farm just down the road from the main farm that Tom and his family had owned and operated for generations. Anne loved the fact that their farm was not visible from the road. That also meant that they had a very long, winding gravel driveway. A beautiful mix of pine, maple, and birch trees lined that driveway, adding to the picturesque setting. Anne grabbed the mail from their mailbox and started back to the house.

Is this some kind of cruel joke? Who would send this to me? How did AARP get my name and address? I am not ready for this! These questions and many more stirred up a whirlwind of emotions as Anne opened her mail that fateful afternoon in September. It was, after all, six long months before her 50th birthday.

What has happened to me and my life? I don't look 50, do I? What does this mean for me? Anne wondered how it was possible that she was about to step into the next decade of her life. How did she get to this point? With a cup of coffee in one hand and the envelope welcoming her to AARP in the other, she found a cozy spot on the porch swing and started to think about how she could possibly be headed straight toward her 50th birthday.

"Anne, honey. I'm home! Where are you?" Tom set his worn, dented, and dusty lunch box on the kitchen counter as he had done every day for the past 27 years and began to search for his wife. "There you are! I've been looking all over for you. What's wrong? What's that in your hand?" Anne looked up with tears in her eyes, and Tom's wide smile was quickly replaced with a look of concern. Tom swooped in and wrapped his arms around Anne. After many years of marriage, Tom knew it was better to simply be present with her until she was ready to talk.

Eventually, Anne handed Tom the envelope. He took a deep breath and smiled to himself, relieved when he saw what the envelope contained. "Honey, this is just a mass mailing this company does to build their business. They have some sort of database that gives them the names and addresses of everyone who is about to turn 50, and that triggers the letters to go out. Remember? I got one in the mail last year. The invitation to join their organization isn't really about you; it's simply about them doing business."

"Even if what you say is true, it has really got me thinking about my life. What does this next phase of my life mean for us? For me? I'm going to be 50, and what have I done with my life? What does the future hold? What is my role now that the boys are both married and have families of their own? I'm sorry, I know this sounds silly and that I am overreacting. I'm at a loss. I want to know I have lived God's purpose for me. This invitation to the world of AARP has really sent me into a tailspin. I feel like I'm about to become a card-carrying senior citizen. Oh, I'm sorry Tom. I've been so distracted that I haven't even asked you about your day."

Tom had a deep love and respect for Anne, and it was always hard for him to see her hurt. "Honey, let me get cleaned up. We can jump in the truck and go into town for dinner and afterward take a long walk through Augustine Park."

They had met for the first time at that very park 30 years ago. Tom had been playing in a baseball tournament, and Anne was working in the concession stand. After the last game, Tom and his buddies ordered beer and hotdogs to celebrate their win. Anne caught Tom's eye, and he asked if she would like to meet back at the park later that evening to listen to a Beatles knockoff band that was scheduled to play. Anne said, "I was planning to come back after supper anyway, so maybe I'll see you."

Tom took plenty of ribbing from the guys on the team after they heard him ask Anne out. But he couldn't have cared less! Anne was beautiful and had recently moved back to their hometown. Tom hopped into his 1970 red Chevy pickup and raced home to shower, change, and get back to the park.

"Tommy, you made it home just in time for dinner! I have fried chicken, potato salad, baked beans, and your favorite strawberry pie. Come on, son, join us," his mom insisted.

Beth Williams was known countywide for her amazing ability to whip up a fantastic meal and at the same time keep her five boys in line. Tom, the oldest of the five, had always been very close to both of his parents. He did love his mother's strawberry pie, but there was no time for that tonight.

"Thanks, Mom, but I don't have time to eat. I have to get cleaned up and get back down to the park." Tom grabbed a chicken leg and kissed his mom on the cheek as he raced through the kitchen to his bedroom.

Beth knew her son well, and all indications pointed to his having a date. She quickly grabbed a blanket and threw it in the truck with a note for him and then returned to the supper table.

Stan and Beth, along with Tom's brothers Tyler, James, and the twins, Kyle and Kenny, were finishing dinner when Tom came through the kitchen on his way out. Stan saw Tom rounding the corner and said, "Tommy, where's the fire? You're passing up your mother's fried chicken and strawberry pie just to get back down to the park?" Tom stopped briefly, not knowing what to say because he didn't really want to tell his parents he was meeting a girl.

Then his brothers chimed in with their commentary. Tyler started first, "Geez, Tom, you smell like you used the whole bottle of cologne!"

"She must be half-blind and can't smell if she agreed to go out with you," James added. Then the twins went back and forth with "Tommy's got a girlfriend, Tommy's got a girlfriend."

Stan gave Tom a knowing wink and a smile and said, "Have fun, son," and handed him a $20 bill. "Here's a little extra cash for the night. You did a great job getting the show steers ready for the fair."

Tom was grateful to have a loving family, even if his little brothers were a pain sometimes. He climbed into his truck and found the blanket with this note from his mom: "Bring this along for the concert. She will need something to sit on." Tom smiled and peeled out of the gravel driveway, leaving a trail of dust behind him. He really didn't care about the Beatles or their music, but the idea of meeting up with Anne, maybe getting to slow dance and taking a long walk through the park would be the best way to spend the night.

Anne called her girlfriend Karen as soon as she got home to tell her about Tom asking her out. Karen and Anne had been best friends since the fifth grade and had shared every important event with each other either in person or on the phone. Karen squealed with excitement when Anne told her about the date and demanded to know every detail. After the phone call, Anne got dressed for the evening and told her father she was meeting a friend at the park to listen to the band.

Jacob Miller was happy to have his daughter back home. After his wife died and Anne left for college, it had been too quiet for too long. Anne brought life and energy back to their home. Jacob asked who the friend was, and she told him Tom Williams had asked her to meet him at the park. Jacob knew of the family. They were well known throughout the community for their generosity and fun-loving nature. Stan and Beth Williams, Tom's parents, ran a very successful family beef and crop farm just outside of town. Jacob said, "Please come home after the concert is over and let me know when you get in."

He thought about how Beth Williams had made several meals for them after Linda, Jacob's wife, had passed. Beth's husband, Stan, had a quarter of a steer butchered and delivered to their home to help out during the winter that Linda was sick and Jacob couldn't work. Heck, the Williams boys had dropped off a truckload of wood that winter, too.

Anne and Tom met in the parking lot and parked right next to each other. Anne was in her vintage yellow Volkswagen Beetle and Tom in his red Chevy pickup. Tom grabbed the blanket and suggested they go find a spot to sit and listen to the concert. They headed down a hiking path that led to the clearing where the concert was going to be held. The air was warm with a gentle breeze. The vast variety of wildflowers filled the air with a soft fragrance.

Tom and Anne hit it off right away. They walked and talked until they both noticed the sunset. Tom spread out the blanket so they could stop and take it in. The spot Tom chose overlooked Cedar Lake. Vibrant yellow, orange, pink, and red colors filled the sky as the sun set and reflected perfectly off the still lake. Anne looked even more beautiful to Tom at that moment. Tom noticed that Anne looked a little teary, and he asked her about it.

Anne explained, "It is moments like these when I truly feel the hand of God. He created this evening with the spectacular fireworks show of colors in the sky just for us. He is the one who orchestrated this entire evening. Sometimes it is overwhelming to know just how much I am loved and blessed by my heavenly Father."

Tom was stunned. He had never heard anyone talk so openly about their faith. He certainly didn't expect to hear about Anne's faith on their first date. Anne spoke about her faith much like Tom's grandma Grace did, with an open and honest love and admiration for Jesus. Tom thought, *This is one special girl. This is the girl I am going to marry.*

After the sun slowly set behind the lake, Anne and Tom picked up the blanket and continued walking and talking. The far-off beat of the music could be heard during short pauses in their conversation. Eventually, the music stopped altogether, and they realized the concert had ended. Neither of them wanted the evening to end, but it was time to head back. They sat briefly in a small wooden gazebo, and Tom and Anne shared their first kiss.

That kiss was the beginning of their fantastic journey. Augustine Park and the hiking trail had always been a place of refuge for Tom and for Anne, and it was the perfect place for Tom to take Anne tonight.

Chapter 2

"Anne, that's the third outfit you've tried on. You would look amazing in a gunnysack! Let's go. I'm starving!" Tom pleaded.

Anne turned, ran up the stairs, and returned with the outfit she had originally put on. For their evening walk, she was dressed in a pair of black capris and a pink blouse with a light jacket. "I'm sorry, Tom, it's just, well, nothing seems quite right tonight. I'll grab my purse and meet you in the truck." Anne took a couple of minutes to look in the mirror and adjust her makeup. Her mascara smeared under her eyes as she couldn't stop the tears.

Anne looked in the mirror and said to herself, "What is wrong with you? You are blowing this way out of proportion. Remember, you are a daughter of the most high King." Over the years, Anne had returned to that phrase several times to reframe her thinking. It was something her mother taught her when she was a little girl feeling insignificant and unimportant.

Anne joined Tom, and they rode into town to grab a quick bite and head to the park. They rode in silence as Tom grabbed Anne's hand. Within 15 minutes, they were parked in front of Justine's Diner. It was Tom's favorite place to eat in town. It was as if time stood still there. The diner looked just like it did when Tom and his little brothers rode in the back of their dad's truck to get a root beer float after a day of baling hay. Tom and Anne slid into the booth that wrapped around the speckled aqua-and-black fiberglass table. Justine kept the chrome legs shined to a pristine gleam.

Justine asked from across the diner, "Hey, Tommy, what are you and the missus going to have tonight? I have a meatloaf special with mashed potatoes, gravy, and a slice of apple pie."

"That sounds great to me! What about you, hon?"

Anne thought a minute and answered, "I'll have a piece of that apple pie and a scoop of ice cream."

"You go, girl!" Justine said with amazement. "You are a girl after my own heart! Eat dessert first!"

When their food arrived, Tom commented, "Anne, I am sorry that you are so upset. I haven't seen you eat dessert before a meal since you were pregnant with Clay."

"Part of me thinks I'm being silly, but I can't seem to shake this. Let's talk when we get to the park." Anne took a bite of the warm home-baked apple pie topped with vanilla ice cream softly melting, hoping she could keep it together until they got to the park.

The sun was just beginning to set when they pulled into Augustine Park. Anne slipped on her jacket, and Tom grabbed her hand as they began the hike to their favorite spot. The trail was lined with wood chips, pink and yellow snapdragons, orange daylilies, and deep purple coneflowers. As dusk arrived, the lightning bugs danced across the glade before them. Finally, Anne and Tom arrived at their favorite spot with the view of Cedar Lake and the sun gently dropping from the sky.

"Anne, sweetheart, please talk to me and help me understand what you are going through. It is so hard for me to see you hurting and not be able to do anything about it. Maybe it would help if we started by inviting God into our conversation."

Tom held Anne's hand and prayed, "Heavenly Father, please be with us as we talk and work through what Anne is experiencing. Help Anne feel safe and secure enough to share with me. Lord, help me to be open to truly listen to what she is saying. I ask that you join us both to work through this. You are our strong tower. I ask this in your precious son Jesus's name. Amen."

During the prayer, Anne began to cry. Tom gently wrapped his arms around her and held her until she was ready to talk. Anne began, "Tom, it's not really about that letter from AARP. It just got me thinking about my life and our life together. I am getting older, and I don't know what my purpose is anymore. It seems like my confidence has crumbled, and I feel confused. I haven't felt like this since my mom told me she was sick. Once Mom talked me through coping with her illness and showed me how to lean on my heavenly Father, I was okay. Don't get me wrong, I missed her terribly when she died, and I still do. She taught me how to cope, but somehow those skills seem to have evaporated. I have been praying, but I am still struggling."

Anne continued, "The roles I have had in my life came ready-made with a long to-do list. I had a sense of what to do when we got married and started our family. When I became a mother, the boys needed me for almost everything. I had things to do as they played sports. There was carpooling for practice, tailgating with their friends' parents, and cheering them on from the stands. Then they graduated from high school and went to college. Even then, I still did the cooking and laundry for them. Thank God they found fantastic wives. The boys both moved in to new phases in their lives, which pushed me into a new phase as well. They both have families of their own and don't need me like they did. I don't have anything going on right now. I volunteer a few hours at St. Mary's Hospital, but what is that really? I just push people around in a wheelchair. I don't think there is an easy answer, Tom. I know you are a fixer, but today I need you to do exactly what you are doing right now. Just hold me, listen, and pray. I am grateful that I have you by my side."

Tom softly moved a strand of hair off her flushed face. It had escaped from her ponytail. He whispered, "Anne, I will always be right by your side. I love you. Please promise me you will let me know when there is something I can do."

Anne thought a moment and said, "I will, sweetheart. Let's head back. I'm ready. You, my dear husband, are amazing, and I love you!"

They gathered their things and walked back to the truck, arm in arm. Anne said a silent prayer, thanking her heavenly Father for blessing her with a strong, loving, God-fearing man.

CHAPTER 3

The smell of freshly brewed rich Colombian coffee wafted up the stairs and woke Tom from a deep sleep. This had been their pattern for many years. Anne always got up an hour before anyone else in the house to have quiet time with the Lord. She believed strongly in Proverbs 3:9—*"Honor the Lord with your wealth, with the firstfruits of all your crops."* She used that sacred time, the first hour of her day, to read scripture and pray. After her dedicated time, she brewed a fresh pot of coffee for her and Tom to enjoy.

"Good morning, sweetheart! The coffee smells amazing," Tom said as he took the cup of coffee Anne offered him. "How are you feeling today?"

Anne sighed. "I do feel better after talking with you last night, but I have a ways to go to get back to feeling like myself again. I am going to give Karen a call and see if she has time for lunch or a long conversation over coffee sometime today. After everything we have been through together, I know I can trust her with this and maybe get a little direction."

Tom grabbed his lunch pail, already filled with a fantastic lunch that Anne had prepared for him, as she had for the past 27 years. "I'm glad you are going to reach out to Karen. I am just a phone call away if you need me. Kenny and our boys can take over if you want me to come home."

"Tom, please remind those sons of ours that we have a family cookout on Sunday after church and that I am looking forward to hugging those grandbabies!"

Tom smiled and said, "I sure will, Anne. Don't worry, they will be there."

With that, Tom kissed his wife goodbye and headed out to the farm.

Anne took her cell phone off the charger and called Karen, who picked up immediately and asked, "What's up, girlfriend? You don't usually call this early."

Overcome with emotion, Anne struggled to hold back her tears. When she had composed herself, she asked, "Karen, do you think we could get together for coffee or lunch today? I've been really having a tough time, and I need to talk to my best friend."

"Absolutely! I'll be over in an hour. Then we can decide if you want to go out for coffee or just settle in and talk at your house. Does that sound okay?"

Anne uttered a barely audible "Yup."

"Oh, honey. Remember whose you are, and I'll be over as quick as I can. Love you!" Karen realized right away that her good friend was in trouble and needed her. She cancelled all her appointments for the day, told her husband she was going to spend the day with Anne, and grabbed her Bible, jacket, and a container of freshly baked snickerdoodles before heading out the door.

As Anne hung up the phone, she thought about the remarkable gift of friendship she had in Karen. They had been best friends for years and had shared all life's joys and sorrows together. The Lord had richly blessed their friendship.

Chapter 4

Over the years, Anne and Karen's friendship had experienced extreme highs and lows. For the most part, they had always been there for each other.

Anne's mother, Linda, treated Karen like another daughter. When Linda was diagnosed with cancer and struggled through the treatments, she helped both Anne and Karen turn to Jesus to cope with the changes in her health.

Linda had come to Anne's school concert; it was the last one she would ever attend. The cancer had taken a tremendous toll on Linda. She was very thin and had dark circles under her eyes. She had also lost all her thick, long, auburn hair. A boy at the school made a comment that he thought she looked like the walking dead. Karen heard him and actually punched him. She got detention for that. It was during that time that Karen brought over a dozen colorful scarves for Anne's mom to wear. Linda loved Karen, who ended up staying with Anne the whole week after Linda went to be with Jesus.

Karen was the first person Anne told when Tom asked her to marry him. They pored over bridal magazines and planned the wedding together. Karen was Anne's maid of honor at her wedding. It was a perfect day, and any hiccups along the way were taken care of by Karen and her mom. Anne never knew about anything that went wrong until months after the wedding.

Karen and Jeff were high school sweethearts. They were perfect for each other. Jeff went to seminary while Karen went to the community college to earn a degree in accounting. As soon as Jeff finished seminary, he asked Karen to marry him. Once again, Karen and Anne were poring through bridal magazines and going to bridal shows to learn about the latest wedding trends. Karen, her mom, and Anne put together the most beautiful spring wedding for Karen and Jeff.

But trouble began to brew in Anne and Karen's friendship when the next natural step was to begin a family. They both wanted to have children. Jeff and Karen tried to conceive a full year before Tom and Anne even had thoughts of getting pregnant. However, as soon as they stopped using birth control, Anne was pregnant. Although Karen was happy for them, she was extremely frustrated with not being able to conceive.

As the months went on and Anne's baby bump became obvious, Karen started to avoid her. When they did happen to see each other, Karen made small talk and had a quick excuse to get to another appointment. It was a joy-filled time that Anne couldn't share with her best friend. Not having Karen to share all the special experiences that come with pregnancy and parenthood was especially painful. Many times, she'd pick up the phone to call and then hang up because Karen had stopped taking her calls.

Cade, Anne's firstborn, was born on a beautiful spring morning. He was absolutely perfect—soft wisps of brown hair, huge blue eyes, and his father's grin. His little hand gripped her finger tightly as he nursed easily right from the start. Tom, his family, and Anne's dad filled the hospital room, showering Anne with love. The outpouring of love was wonderful, but Karen's absence was painful. It was a pivotal time in Anne's life that she could not share with her lifelong friend.

Karen and Anne rarely saw each other after Cade's birth. Jeff called Anne and said he simply couldn't get Karen to reconnect with her even though Karen admitted that was exactly what she needed to do. Her infertility and the depression that followed proved to be too much for her to deal with alone. Karen and Jeff sought out a Christian counselor to help her grieve the loss of never being able to give birth to a child of their own.

Two years later, the Lord blessed Tom and Anne with another picture-perfect baby boy. Clay was born with auburn-colored hair, the same color as Anne's mother's hair. He weighed 9 pounds 4 ounces and was 21 inches long. When the nurse handed Clay to Tom, he took Clay in his arms, gazed into his huge brown eyes, and said, "Anne, I think we have another little farmer!"

Two weeks after Clay was born, Karen called. "Anne, this is Karen. I know this call has been way overdue. If you can find it in your heart to forgive me, I'd like to come over to see you and the boys. Maybe we can begin to mend our friendship—if you are willing."

"I would love to see you, Karen! I have missed you terribly. Come right over. Beth is here helping out, so the house looks good, but I haven't had much sleep, so no promises on how I look."

Beth brewed a fresh pot of coffee for Karen and Anne and set out some of her freshly baked cookies on a decorative plate. Karen arrived 30 minutes later with flowers for Anne and gifts for both boys. Shortly after Karen met the boys, Beth took them both into the nursery so Karen and Anne could talk.

Once Beth and the boys were upstairs and safely in the nursery, both Anne and Karen began to talk at the same time.

"No, Anne, please let me go first, or I might lose the courage that has taken me months to grow." Tears streamed down both Karen's and Anne's faces as Karen talked about the frustration, depression, and jealousy she struggled with as she went through months of infertility and then the in vitro fertilization treatments. "I had hoped we could get pregnant without any medical intervention. Then I thought I would definitely get pregnant through IVF. I know this sounds silly, but I thought if we had motherhood in common, things would get better between us. When that didn't happen, I lost it. Jeff couldn't get me to get out of bed for months. Finally, my mom and Jeff got me to go to counseling. I started seeing a Christian counselor, a member of our church family, and slowly things have been starting to turn around. I have been seeing her for about six months now. Through prayer and talking things out, I realized I had resentments toward you that had nothing to do with you. I blamed God and Jeff and, well, anyone within swinging distance. I am so sorry, and I hope that someday you can forgive me. I haven't been there for you during a time I'm sure you could have used a friend. Please forgive me, Anne."

Through the tears, Anne told her dear friend, "Of course I forgive you. Promise me we will never again allow this much time to go by without talking to each other. I don't think I could take it."

"Two days maximum without talking, I promise, even when we are on vacation. Wow! Look at us. We are one big, wet, snotty mess! I am so relieved that you have forgiven me. Now, do you think it would be okay if I held that new little baby of yours?"

As if on cue, Beth rounded the corner with the boys and handed little Clay to Karen. Cade crawled up into Anne's lap and demanded that his momma read him *The Poky Little Puppy* for what seemed like the 100th time.

"Well, ladies, it looks like the two of you have things handled. I am going to run home and get lunch on the table for my hungry boys!" Beth gave both of the women a hug and a kiss on the cheek. "It is so good to see you together again. You two are like bookends. It's just not right when one of you is missing."

CHAPTER 5

Sleep did not come easily for Anne last night, even though she had a good talk with Tom that evening. She was so grateful that her best friend Karen was always there for her. They enjoyed a special bond and level of understanding that only trusted, lifetime friends experience.

Anne greeted Karen at the door with a cup of coffee. They hugged and went out to the back porch to talk.

"Karen, this might sound absolutely crazy to you, but I have been floundering. I feel like I don't really have a purpose anymore. I guess when I got the letter in the mail from AARP, I started to think about my life and what my role is. I am getting older, and my roles aren't the same anymore. They aren't clearly defined like they once were. The boys have their wives and their own children. Tom, Kenny, and the boys run the farm. Jeff's sermon last Sunday got me thinking about things, too. He asked the congregation what we were each doing to advance the kingdom. Wow! Just listening to myself tell you what has been going on in my head is a big mess of everything." Anne slid back in the swing and stared off toward the pond.

Karen had a knack of knowing Anne's moods and the best way to approach her. She reached out to Anne and took her hand, praying, "Dear heavenly Father, I invite you into our conversation right now.

Please be with us both as we talk about becoming old ladies." Anne snickered. "In all seriousness, Lord, be with us and help us both see how we have advanced your kingdom and how we can continue to do good work to glorify you. It is in your precious son Jesus's name we pray. Amen."

Anne couldn't contain her laughter any longer and busted loose with a belly laugh. Karen acted innocent and then said with a little grin, "Sorry, sister, but it was getting a little too serious. And besides, I think God enjoys a good laugh as much as the next person."

"That felt so good to just laugh. But what do you think? Am I going through a midlife crisis? If I am, how do I get through it?" Anne asked.

"Not to pour salt in your wounds, but technically, I think you are too old for a midlife crisis."

"Karen, you are too much! You know you are the only person who can shoot right through my little pity party and help me get right to the heart of the matter."

"Anne, if you want to look back over our lives together, we can identify all the kingdom work you have been involved in. There are also lots of things you can do in your current circumstances that will lend itself to a deeper connection with the Lord." Karen was on the edge of her deck chair as she began to go over some of the amazing life events they had gone through together with the ever-present hand of the Lord being with them.

"Remember how your mom sat us both down to tell us about her cancer diagnosis? I had never been more scared and honored at the same time in my entire life," recalled Karen.

"I can still remember both of us upstairs in my bedroom applying the makeup you took from your mom's drawer. We thought we looked so grown-up with baby-blue eye shadow filling the entire space between our eyebrows and eyelashes! Then there was the blush that we brushed in an upward stroke just like our *Seventeen* magazine suggested. Then it was time for us to put on the ruby-red lipstick. We were a sight," Anne reminisced.

"The fashion-forward fun came to a screeching halt when your mom called us downstairs. She sounded so serious that I was sure my mom had called yours about the missing makeup. If nothing else, I think our new look lightened your mom's mood, if only for a moment," Karen added.

"That's right. She took one look at the two of us, busted out laughing, and asked us to wash off our 'war paint' so we could talk," Anne remembered.

The memory of their first experiment with makeup and the conversation that followed remained as clear and poignant as the day it happened. Anne had no idea that day that her entire world was about to be turned upside down. Anne's mom had news that neither of the girls expected to hear.

"Anne, there is something serious I need to talk to you about. Karen, you may as well hear it, too, since the two of you are as close to sisters as you could possibly be without actually being related by blood." Linda then had the girls sit down on the sofa, and she sat across from them on the footstool.

Linda began. "Girls, I just got some test results back from the doctor, and I have breast cancer. The doctor thinks I may have had it for a while. There is treatment; they call it chemotherapy. I start tomorrow. Unfortunately, the treatment will make me sick, and my hair will fall out. The doctors don't know a lot about this disease. It isn't contagious. I may as well let you know that your dad is not taking the news well. Please be gentle and patient with him until he can come to grips with everything that is happening. You can ask me anything about what is going to happen, and I will be open and honest with you."

Anne and Karen both started to cry. Linda grabbed both of their hands and said, "Girls, we need to pray. This is scary only because there are a lot of unknowns. Our heavenly Father knows everything. He will not leave us and will be a huge comfort to us."

"Dear Lord," Linda prayed, "protect these beautiful girls and let them feel your comfort and strength as we go through this illness together. I pray for your healing hand to be upon me. Lord, please be with the doctors and nurses as they treat the cancer. Heavenly Father, I surrender to your will. Amen."

Anne timidly asked with a quivering lip and trembling voice, "Mom, does this mean you are going to die?"

"Aw, come here, sweetie."

Anne climbed onto her petite mother's lap and wept. Linda gently rocked her daughter as she had many years ago after a skinned knee. "Anne, the Lord has a plan for each of us, and only he knows the plan. Someday, when we are all in heaven together, we may find out the answers. It isn't important to ask why. It is far more important that we focus on enjoying each day and praise God for every day he gives us to be together in this world. You know our days on earth are numbered. How soon it will happen for each of us is not in our hands. I love you completely, my dear Anne. As much as we love each other, God's love for each of us is limitless and deeper than we can imagine. Trust in the Lord."

Eventually, Linda told the girls she was going to lie down for a nap and that they should go back upstairs and work on perfecting their new look.

With heavy hearts, Anne and Karen went back upstairs.

Over the next six months, Linda put up a valiant fight against the cancer. During that time, she had a double mastectomy, chemotherapy, and radiation treatments. Anne's father, Jacob, took a leave of absence from the fire department. Linda was too weak to drive herself to the medical appointments, and Jacob wanted her to use the little bit of energy she had to get better. Their church community came together and brought food, cut the grass, and, with the first snowfall, shoveled the drive and sidewalks for them.

Over time, Linda, Jacob, and Anne learned to cope as best they could with the ups and downs of their journey with cancer. There were times when the cancer went into remission, but it seemed to come back worse than it was the time before. The day after Linda shared her diagnosis with the girls, she started a Bible study with Anne and sometimes Karen. It was crucial to Linda that Anne know the Lord and learn to rely on her heavenly Father. Although always hopeful, Linda had a feeling that she would be meeting Jesus sooner rather than later. Anne loved reading the Bible with her mom. She always felt comforted, and it was exciting to know the Lord whom her mother trusted completely.

Just days before her death, Linda called Anne to her side. "Sweetheart, the Lord is calling me home. I am going to go be with Jesus. He has prepared a place for me. I need you to know that I will be in his glorious presence, and I will not have pain any longer."

"But Mom, what about that experimental treatment Dad talked about yesterday?" Anne asked.

"Your father desperately wants me to live, and I love him for that, but my time here is nearly over. No extra treatments are going to change that. I am so grateful for the time we have had to love, laugh, and worship God together. I know you are going to miss me, and that is natural. I also know that you have developed an amazing relationship with our heavenly Father. He will carry you through the difficult days to come. Pray throughout the day and before you go to bed. I haven't been able to get your dad to lean on our Savior through this, so I know it will be even harder on him. Remember to pray for your dad. I love you with my whole heart, Anne." Then Anne slipped into bed with her mom, and they cuddled until Linda fell asleep.

Linda never regained consciousness and lived for another three days. Anne prayed over her mother. Karen joined her in some of the prayers as did their pastor. In her last few hours, Linda's respirations slowed, and she ever so gently left this world to be with her Savior.

Anne experienced an odd sense of peace with her mother's passing. She knew her mom was in a better place. Jacob, however, was inconsolable. He was racked with guilt over not pursuing alternative treatments sooner for Linda's cancer. He hadn't been willing to join Linda and Anne in their Bible studies and wouldn't pray with them, either. He was incredibly angry with God. In fact, if Linda hadn't preplanned her funeral with the help of Anne, Karen, and Karen's mom, the funeral would not have been in a church or had a pastor officiating.

Jacob returned to his job at the fire department a week after the funeral. His fellow firefighters welcomed him back, first with sorrowful hugs and then with hearty slaps on the back and friendly banter. Jacob was a huge asset to the department and had been sorely missed over the past several months. It was a relief for him to see his friends and climb into his old bunk. He hadn't been able to bring himself to sleep in the bed he had shared with Linda.

Jacob let his thoughts drift to his daughter, Anne. She seemed to be handling Linda's death very well. Sure, she was sad, but she was continuing on with her life just as Linda had hoped she would. Maybe all that praying and reading from the Bible had helped Anne cope.

Jacob returned home after his 48-hour shift to find Anne sitting at the kitchen table reading her Bible and sipping a Coke. "Hey, sunshine! How was your day?"

"It was good, Dad. Each day is a little easier. Don't get me wrong, I miss Mom terribly, but I know she is in heaven with Jesus and no longer in pain."

"Anne, I have to be honest, I don't understand any of that. It doesn't make any sense to me that God would take a beautiful wife and mother away from her family when they need her." Jacob gazed out the window, looking at nothing in particular.

"Dad, sit down. I want to share something with you. I have accepted Jesus as my Lord and Savior. God sent his only Son to earth to pay the cost of my sins so I can have a relationship with my heavenly Father. I read Mom's Bible every day to learn more about him and the life he wants me to live. It also helps me to feel close to Mom."

Anne continued, "Dad, I don't know why Mom was called to go home to Jesus when she was, but God knows. Someday we will all be together again in heaven, and it will be spectacular. Imagine reuniting with Mom when she isn't in any pain."

"Anne, I'm glad you had a special relationship with your mom. It sounds like you have found comfort in your heavenly Father, and I'm happy about that. But I'm not ready to get into that right now."

"Mom told me you would have a hard time understanding. That's okay, Dad. I love you and so does Jesus. He will always be there for you. When you are ready to accept him into your heart, you will have an amazing peace that I know you can't even imagine right now."

"Okay, okay, that's enough of that for now. I stopped by Justine's and picked up supper. Why don't you clear off the table and set it. I'm going to get cleaned up, and we can have Justine's famous fried chicken and mashed potatoes."

As soon as Anne was sure her dad was in the shower, she called Karen. "Karen, guess what? I shared the gospel with Dad tonight!"

"Oh my gosh! How did it go?" Karen asked, knowing it wouldn't be easy for Anne to share or for her dad to hear.

"Well, he heard me out. I did my part, and now the rest is up to him and the Holy Spirit."

"That is fantastic! Maybe your mom was right, that it is just going to take time for your dad to accept Jesus as his Lord and Savior. I think it's cool that the very first person you shared the gospel with was your dad."

Anne added a prayer of thanksgiving that night that her father had been willing to at least hear what she had to say about salvation.

CHAPTER 6

The sweet and spicy aroma of Karen's snickerdoodles filled the air as she opened the seal of the Tupperware container. Karen took two of the delicate cinnamon delights and handed the bowl to Anne.

"You know what? I'm not even going to pretend I shouldn't eat these. I love your snickerdoodles, and I can't think of a better time to have a few than right now." Anne grabbed some cookies. The coffee and cookies were an amazing combination.

"You mentioned that you think you haven't really done anything all that significant when it comes to kingdom work. We just talked about how you shared the gospel with your dad. I remember another time when your belief and strength through Jesus really helped Tom and his family."

"I'm sorry, but I can't think of any time I was able to help Tom and his family. They are super strong in their faith," Anne said.

"What about when Tom's brother James was killed in that farming accident?"

"I guess we all have tiptoed around that memory. He was such a great guy. Tom and I had only been married a month when it happened." Anne sighed as she remembered that fateful night.

The sights, sounds, and smells of that horrendous event came crashing to the forefront of Anne's mind. The pit in her stomach when she received the call to come to the hospital, the antiseptic smell that engulfed her as she rushed through the emergency room doors, and the utter devastation the unexpected death of a loved one brought to the family and community were staggering.

"Anne, I'm going to grab a quick bite and head back out to the farm. Dad, James, and I are going to work as long as we can to get the last of the corn off the fields before the snow starts tomorrow. It will be late but so worth it. I will have lots of time to spend with my beautiful bride when the fall harvest is done!" Tom winked at Anne as he sat down and practically inhaled the supper Anne had carefully prepared. Beth had given Anne a handmade cookbook chock-full of her time- and taste-tested recipes. Beth starred the recipes that Tom liked best. The meal she made that night was one of his favorites.

Tom got up from the table, kissed Anne on the forehead and said, "That was better than Mom's!" Tom was out the door and down the driveway before Anne had a chance to finish her meal.

Anne cleared the table, put the leftovers in the refrigerator, and washed the dishes. She was glad to make meals that Tom enjoyed. Then she sat down with her Bible to work on her latest Bible study. Before she started, Anne said a prayer of gratitude. The first month of their marriage had been amazing. Even though Tom was busy on the farm, he always made time for her. She had a mother-in-law that treated her like the daughter she never had.

Anne was about an hour into her study when the call came. It was Dr. Sorkin from St. Amelia's Hospital emergency room.

"This is Dr. Sorkin from St. Amelia's ER. May I speak to Anne Williams?" the voice on the line asked.

"This is Anne Williams. What can I do for you, Dr. Sorkin?"

"Mrs. Williams, your husband Tom asked me to call you. There has been a farming accident. Tom wasn't hurt. It was his brother James. Tom would like you to come to the hospital immediately."

Anne knew it had to be very serious if she had gotten a call from the ER doctor and not from the family. Fear started to creep into her body and choke her throat. She swallowed hard and pleaded, "What happened? Can I speak to Tom?"

"I'm sorry, Mrs. Williams. I can't disclose that information over the phone. Please get here as quickly as you can."

Anne hung up the phone and dropped to her knees, crying out to Jesus and asking him to be with her on her trip to the hospital and to embrace the family with his love, comfort, and healing. She then grabbed her purse, hopped into her Volkswagen, and drove to the hospital. When she pulled into the emergency room parking lot, she saw all the family vehicles there, along with Pastor Mike's car.

Anne ran into the reception area and asked for James Williams's room. The nurse came from behind the desk and walked Anne to the chapel. There, Anne found her strong, handsome husband sobbing, with arms around his little brothers Kyle and Kenny who were inconsolable. Beth and Stan were talking with Pastor Mike. It was obvious that they, too, had been crying. Tom looked up and saw Anne standing in the entrance of the chapel.

"Oh, Anne, I'm so glad you're here," Tom sobbed.

"Tom, honey, what in the world happened?"

"No one told you? James was killed in an accident tonight. He was trying to unclog the head of the combine and was pulled into it." With that, Tom broke down again.

"It's all my fault. If I hadn't been in such a damn hurry to get the corn off the field, none of this would have happened. If only I could go back in time and undo this day." Tom turned and kicked the door.

"It's not your fault, Tom. If I had shown up for work like I was supposed to, James wouldn't have been driving the combine, much less trying to fix it." Tyler was racked with guilt for blowing off the last night of harvest. He hadn't called to say he was going to be late, nor did he answer when his dad called looking for him. When Tyler didn't show, James jumped in the combine to finish up.

James was excited to finish harvesting the last of the corn when he noticed that the teeth that pulled the corn stalks into the combine were jammed up with a bunch of stalks, not allowing the corn to move through the machine. He jumped off the combine, thinking he could simply kick the stalks loose and keep going. However, he failed to shut off the combine, and when the stalks where loosened, the teeth reengaged and caught his boot, pulling him into the unrelenting and unforgiving machine.

James was nearly done with the last field when the combine head got clogged and stopped working. Tom had just left the field with two gravity boxes filled with corn. He was heading back to the grain dryer, which was manned by their father. Kenny and Kyle unhooked the gravity boxes for Tom, and he went back to the field to wait for James to fill the last gravity box with corn. When Tom pulled into the field, he noticed the combine was stopped. The combine never stopped in the field unless it was broken down or stuck. Tom thought, *Great, the combine breaks down with just two passes left to finish up our entire fall harvest.* He pulled up next to the combine to help James work on the mammoth machine. Tom climbed out of his tractor and immediately knew something was very wrong. He couldn't find James. Then he walked around the front of the combine and saw that his brother had been pulled into the head of the combine. The sight was horribly gruesome. Tom yelled at the top of his lungs and desperately tried to free James from the huge machine that had engulfed him. Quickly Tom realized that his efforts were futile. He pulled out his mobile phone and called his father.

Tom drew in a deep breath and said, "Dad, call an ambulance out to the field and come out here right away. Don't let Mom or the boys come. It's James, he . . . he's dead, Dad." Tom couldn't keep it together any longer, and he sat down next to where his sweet brother's mangled body was lodged in the machinery and sobbed. He cried out to Jesus for a miracle—anything.

After what seemed like an eternity, Tom heard the familiar roar of his father's one-ton pickup. It came to a stop, and Stan ran over to his son. "Tommy, what happened?"

"I don't know, Dad. This is what I saw when I pulled in to get the last of the grain. For the love of God, can we please get him out of there?"

"We can't do it alone. Call the fire department and let them know we need the Jaws of Life to get Jimmy out of there." That was all Stan could take, and he walked around the combine and vomited. The silence that followed was broken by Stan's guttural cries. Tom ran around and held his father as he grieved the loss of his third-born son. James was 18.

CHAPTER 7

The once rowdy, full-of-laughter exuberance of Stan and Beth Williams fell silent as the family tried to figure out how they were going to go on without James. A huge shadow loomed over Tom and Anne's marriage of just one month. Tom had become silent and stoic as he tended to all the duties on the farm.

As Anne and Tom were getting ready for the funeral, Anne asked Tom to sit down next to her on the bed. "Tom, I can't possibly know the pain you are going through right now. I want to walk through this with you, but we need to talk about it for that to happen."

"What do you want me to say, Anne? I blame myself for James's death, and so do my dad and Tyler. We are all a wreck, barely holding on." Tom fought back the tears as he spoke and turned away from Anne.

Anne reached for Tom's hand and said, "Tom, the Lord took James home. It was way earlier than any of us would have ever imagined. It wouldn't have mattered if Tyler was there or if you weren't in a hurry to get the crops off or if your dad was doing the combining. It simply was his time. It isn't rational in a worldly perspective at all. My heart is breaking for James. I loved him, too. I believe he is with my mom in heaven. Will you pray with me, sweetheart?"

Tom kneeled in front of his wife with tears streaming down his face. "Yes, Anne, please. I can't deal with this alone any longer."

"Dearest heavenly Father. Lord, please wrap your loving arms around the Williams family and their friends. You are the great comforter and strong tower. Help them know they can run to you and you will accept them with open arms. We are all hurting so much that it is hard to breathe. Lord, help Tom, Tyler, and Stan forgive themselves. This tragedy was not their doing. I pray that you unite our hearts as a family with the precious Lord Jesus in the center of the family and the center of Tom's and my marriage. Comfort us, Lord, and give us peace. I ask this all in your precious son Jesus's name. Amen."

Tom laid his head in Anne's lap and wept. She gently stroked his hair and continued to pray for her handsome new groom whose pain was so raw and intense that he could hardly bear it.

The funeral was held in the high school field house. All the high school students and the rest of the community attended the service to mourn and pay their respects to the Williams family. Stan and Beth stood next to the table with hundreds of treasured pictures of James and the urn that held his ashes. His graduation picture was enlarged and placed on a tripod at the front of the field house. Tom and Anne, Tyler, Kyle, and Kenny formed a line next to Stan and Beth, greeting everyone as they passed by.

Pastor Mike gave an inspirational message during the service. Beth heard Anne praying softly during the silent prayer. Tom seemed slightly more relaxed, but Tyler and the twins could hardly stay in their seats. This was all too much for them. Beth recognized Anne's inner peace and remembered that Anne had dealt with her mother's death five years earlier.

A few days after the funeral, Anne found herself seated at Beth's dining room table reading through hundreds of sympathy cards.

They took turns reading each card aloud and then responded with a thank-you card.

"Anne, I can't thank you enough for coming over and helping me wade through all these cards. When I looked at the pile, it was a bit overwhelming. I'm so glad to be doing this with you."

Anne smiled and said, "I'm glad to be here with you. All these cards represent hundreds of people whose lives were touched by James. What a privilege to have known and loved him. Now we have the honor to respond to the people who cared about him."

"Anne, dear, can I ask you something?" Beth asked timidly. "I mean, well, if it's too personal, you can tell me."

"Ask me anything, Beth. What's on your mind?"

"Well, I noticed during the silent prayer at the funeral that you were softly praying to yourself. You also seem to have a peace about James's passing that, well, the rest of us don't have. At first, I thought it might be because you haven't known him as long as we all have. But then I also know that you loved him as if he were your brother. I have noticed that Tom is doing better, too. How have you come to have peace about James's passing?"

"It's my relationship with Jesus Christ and accepting him as my Savior that has made all of the difference for me. Beth, when my mom got sick with cancer, she tried to cram a lifetime with me into what little time she had left. Mom loved the Lord and lived to glorify him. She used every opportunity she had to teach me about the Lord, develop a relationship with Jesus, and learn to lean on and trust in my heavenly Father. My dad didn't handle Mom's illness very well, and she knew he would struggle, so she wanted me to be able to trust in my heavenly Father. I have a deep abiding love of the Lord, and he is right by my side in the good times and the bad. I turned to Jesus during this super-hard time in my life, and I have been praying for Tom and the whole Williams family. The Lord will get us through this."

Beth thought about what Anne shared. She did remember Linda's struggle with cancer and Jacob's relentless pursuit of new treatments to help save her. Beth looked over to Anne and said, "I'm so sorry, dear. This is not your first go-round with a devastating loss."

"No, it isn't, but that doesn't make it hurt less. What does help me is my strong belief that God has a specific plan for each one of us. Our days are numbered in his book. Those are just a couple of the lessons Mom taught Karen and me. I like to think that there is a little bit of her that lives on in me, especially when I share my faith."

"You have become an amazing example of faith in action. Keep praying for us, honey. The sorrow really hasn't gotten much better. Tyler and Kyle have refused to go back to work on the farm. It just hurts too much for them to go out there knowing James is gone. Tyler is applying for jobs in town, and Kyle has been spending a lot of time in his room. That leaves Tommy, Stan, and Kenny to pick up the slack. It isn't easy for them, either, but the work has to get done," Beth shared with resignation.

"Of course, I will continue to pray. Have you and Stan thought about talking to Pastor Mike? He might be able to help in ways that neither of us can think of. He came over a couple of times to talk with Mom and me. Dad didn't want to be part of our talks, but it really helped us. Maybe the boys would be willing to talk to Pastor Mike, too."

Beth thought a minute and said, "You know these Williams men, they are pretty tight lipped when they are hurting. I know they're as miserable as I am."

Beth got up from the table and walked over to the picture window that overlooked the fenced-in field of majestic black Angus cattle leisurely grazing in the emerald-green pasture. She softly wept as she thought of the countless times James was out in that very pasture chasing cattle, practicing roping, and sometimes amazing his little brothers by balancing on top of the wooden fence while walking the length of it.

Beth dabbed her eyes, turned to Anne, smiled weakly, and said, "Excuse me, Anne. I have a call to make to a certain Pastor Mike."

Pastor Mike was more than happy to help the Williams family navigate their grief. It started slowly with Beth and the pastor meeting alone. Then Stan, out of curiosity about his wife's improved mood, joined her in talking about their pain. Eventually, the boys came to a couple of family sessions, and the Williamses began the process of knitting their family back together. They would never be the family they had been, but they grew stronger through it all.

CHAPTER 8

"Wow, Karen! I hadn't thought about that in a very long time. That was such a long time ago and a very dark time for the family," Anne said as her mind drifted back to the year they had lost James.

"Harvest time is always bittersweet. The family reaps the benefit of a year's worth of hard work, but everyone has James on their minds."

"If you ask me, Anne, it was your grace, love, and patience that helped the family persevere that first year after James died. How many new brides could have dealt with all that pain and hurt during the first year of their marriage? Your brother-in-law was killed, your honeymoon plans were cancelled, Tom was silent most of the time, and everyone was walking on eggshells. You, my friend, stayed right by Tom's side and never wavered.

"You were right alongside me during that time, too," Anne continued as she reached for another cookie. "Remember how many times we prayed together, asking for comfort and healing? I have always had God and you with me."

Anne wondered out loud, "But that was all a very long time ago, Karen. That all seems so very far away. What about my life now?"

"You really are having a tough time, aren't you, Anne? We are not going to skip from then to now without going over a few more pivotal times where your influence, patience, and faith touched other people's lives."

Karen added, "Let's talk about us. It was your patience, faithfulness, and willingness to forgive me that has allowed us to remain best friends. I was overcome with insane jealousy when you got pregnant twice and Jeff and I couldn't get pregnant. I was horrible to you, my very best friend. It probably would have been easier for you to never speak to me again."

"Karen, I have to admit that it hurt deeply to not go through my pregnancies with you. We had shared everything big and small for many years. I was hurt and angry for a while, but mostly I was really heartbroken. When you were ready to talk, I was a little apprehensive. I didn't want you to come into my life and then leave again. You were incredibly brave to make that call and bare your soul. I missed you so terribly that I would never have turned you away. I was and am so blessed to have you back in my life. I think the Holy Spirit was working through both of us then. He softened both of our hearts, and it was time for us to be friends again."

"Isn't it ironic that we both went through those years of extreme sadness, my infertility, your pregnancies, and joy without each other? As hard as it was, it forced us to rely on our heavenly Father because we didn't have each other."

Anne added, "I don't want you to feel guilty about that time in our lives. You were going through a terrible time of frustration and grief. I had two healthy babies and the love and support of Tom and his family. Even Dad would stop by to make sure I was doing okay. Having you back in my life and the boys' lives has been fantastic! You know they love their auntie Karen!"

"You bet they do," Karen insisted.

"Are you up for a walk?" Anne asked. "Tom told me the late wildflowers are still blooming along the hiking trail."

CHAPTER 9

The hiking trail was bursting with spectacular color. The Black-eyed Susans dotted either side of the path. Tangerine-colored daylilies, daisies, and purple coneflowers added dimension to the beauty.

"It is incredible out here," Karen commented. "I don't know how you get anything done. I would be so distracted with these trails that I wouldn't find my way back to the house until nightfall."

Anne smiled. "I agree. It is amazing! Honestly, sometimes I do spend the day just wandering around out here. We extended the hiking paths so we now have about five miles of meandering trails. Tom actually planted some of the wildflowers. He is so sweet. I am one lucky girl to have him as my husband!"

Karen pointed to a little garden area and asked, "What's that?"

"Let me show you. Tom created this oasis for us years ago. Actually, he put it together when Clay was six months old."

On their way to the garden was a trellis shaped in an 8-foot-tall arch. Winding around the arch was a bounty of fragrant pink country roses. As they walked under the roses into a small clearing, there was a white glider rocker for two, a small table, and a sign posted on a birch tree that provided shade over the rocker. The sign read, "1 Earth, 6 Oceans, 7 Continents, 195 Countries, 7 Billion People. . .and somehow we met. . .a miracle meant to be. —Author Unknown"

"Anne, I love this spot! Now I remember when Tom came to Jeff and asked for some help creating this for you."

"Well, that was a time in my life that I'm not too proud of." Anne sighed. "I never had postpartum depression with Cade, but after Clay was born, it hit me hard. I had no idea what happened to me, but the heavy weight of depression was like a dark, stormy cloud always hanging over me.

"Now that I think about it, your coming back into my life was exactly what I needed in many ways. I had been feeling sad after Clay was born, but within a month, I couldn't get out of bed, and I was exhausted. I was so confused because the heaviness of the depression came at a time when I should have been super excited. I mean, I had my boys and a loving husband, and my best friend was back, for Pete's sake! You were a lifesaver."

Karen and Anne sat down on the glider, recalling the depression that seemed to have settled in on Anne and wouldn't let go.

CHAPTER 10

It had been three weeks since Clay was born, and Anne seemed to have less energy now than the day they had brought him home. Tom noticed that Anne was often distracted and seemed to be in her own world much of the time. Anne grew increasingly weary and less able to keep up with the most basic tasks. Tom was able to finish work early one day and came home to spend a little extra time with Anne and the boys.

Tom searched the house looking for them and eventually found them in the bedroom. Little Cade was playing with his trucks on the bed next to Anne. The baby was crying in the bassinet, and Anne was sleeping.

"Anne, wake up! Clay is crying his little eyes out, and Cade is playing trucks while you sleep. What is wrong with you?" Tom demanded.

"What, what are you talking about, and why are you yelling?" Anne asked, trying to shake the sleepiness out of her head.

"Something is seriously wrong. In the past, you have always been a hypervigilant mom. Now you don't seem to care about anyone or anything other than sleeping. I'm sure the baby has added a lot of extra stress, but this is really getting out of hand. The house is a mess, the kids are out of diapers, Clay needs to be fed, and Cade cannot watch himself. Honey, if you need help, I can have my mom come over and give you a hand. She has been offering to help out. I have to work, Anne, and something has got to change. This isn't safe."

Anne burst into tears. "Tom, I feel terrible. I'm afraid there is something wrong with me. I feel so ashamed that I am letting you and the boys down. I have no energy or appetite. I haven't accepted your mom's offers to help because I feel so inept. I don't want her to think I can't take care of you and the boys. My milk is beginning to dry up, and I don't think I have enough to keep little Clay satisfied anymore. I'm such a failure as a mother and wife."

"Whoa, whoa, whoa! Nobody said you are a failure as a mother or wife. Let's get that straight right now." Tom grabbed his now sobbing wife and wrapped his arms around her. He gently suggested, "Sweetheart, I don't know much about this, but is it possible that you have some sort of hormone imbalance after having the baby that is causing the trouble you're having? Would you be willing to go see Dr. Benton tomorrow? None of this is like you, so I think it has to be something else."

Anne nodded her head yes and said, "It would be a relief to find out if I have something else going on. Do you think you could get your mom to watch the boys?"

"Try to keep her away! Mom and Dad have been dying to have some grandparent time with the boys. Now, what can I do to help right now?"

That afternoon, Tom ran Anne a warm bath and sent her into the bathroom for a long soak. While Anne was in the bath, he fed the boys lunch, cleaned up the kitchen, and folded some laundry. He also made a call to Anne's gynecologist, Dr. Benton. He was able to schedule an appointment for the next day at 11:00 a.m.

"Hey, Mom, do you think you and Dad could take care of the boys tomorrow?" Tom asked.

"Well of course, Tommy. Is everything okay?" Beth could always tell when something was wrong with one of her boys, and Tom was certainly no exception.

"Honestly, Mom, things are not going very well with Anne. I'm not sure what's going on, but she is not herself at all. When I got home this afternoon, I couldn't find her. Eventually, I found Anne and the boys in our bedroom with Cade playing trucks on the bed, Anne sound asleep, and the baby crying in the bassinet. I don't think she has changed her clothes in a couple days. I'm really worried. We have an appointment to see Dr. Benton tomorrow, and hopefully we can get to the bottom of this."

"Tommy, it is not all that uncommon for women to go through a type of depression after childbirth. I have a hunch that might be what is going on with Anne. The poor dear; I bet she is feeling just awful. I'll tell you what. Dad and I will come over to your house to watch the boys. That way I can make a few meals, clean, and do some laundry. It will make it easier for Anne when you two come home," Beth offered.

"That sounds great! My next call is to the pediatrician. I am going to run into town and pick up whatever formula she suggests and some diapers. I'll get carryout for supper and head home. Tell Dad I'll be over for chores in the morning, but I'll be gone for the rest of the day. Our appointment is at 11:00." Tom was grateful for such loving and understanding parents.

"I'm on it, Tommy. Dad and I will be praying for Anne, you, and the boys."

"It's funny, that's usually what Anne is saying to everyone else." Tom sighed.

"Everything is going to be okay. You are doing everything you can to fix the situation. We are a family, and family faces problems together," Beth firmly stated.

"Thanks, Mom! See you tomorrow at our house by 10:00 a.m."

"Bye, Tommy."

It was difficult for Beth to hear the pain and concern in her son's voice. She was confident that they could come together to support Anne until she was feeling like herself again. Beth took a chicken out of the freezer. As soon as it thawed, she would cook it to make several meals for Tom and his family.

Anne finished her bath and got dressed. She had a little more color, and it was nice to see her dressed. She took a bottle of water out of the fridge and sat down at the kitchen table.

"Did you get a hold of your mom?" Anne asked weakly.

"I did, and she practically jumped through the phone at the opportunity to watch the kids! Anne, let's run into town. We can stop by the store and get a few groceries, pick up some supper, and maybe show off the boys a little!" Tom hoped Anne would agree to go with him.

"You can go, Tom. I'll stay back with the boys. I don't feel like going out tonight."

"Come on, Anne, it will be good for you to get out of the house and take in some fresh air. Just come along. If you want to stay in the truck, you can, but grab your shoes and let's get going. The sooner we leave, the sooner we can get back."

Anne finally agreed to ride along. "Tom, I hate to admit this, but we will have to pick up some formula for the baby. I'll use it to supplement the breastfeeding. I hope it will just be temporary."

"I have a call in to the pediatrician asking about formula. I thought it might relieve some pressure for you until you are feeling better. I hope you don't mind," Tom added gently.

A tear fell down Anne's face as she said, "I just can't do this right now. Thank you for taking care of it."

With the boys strapped in their car seats, Tom and Anne headed into town. Anne stared out the window at nothing in particular. Both boys fell asleep less than a mile from home. Tom was beginning to feel better just knowing they had a plan of attack for whatever had been happening with his young family. They ran all the errands and were back home within two hours.

Anne nursed Clay and finished the feeding with a bottle of formula. Tom fed Cade, read him a story, and rocked him to sleep. Both Tom and Anne fell into bed exhausted with the hope that tomorrow would be a better day.

Stan and Beth arrived the next morning with several meals Beth intended to tuck away in the freezer after Tom and Anne left for the doctor. Anne gave Beth instructions for the boys' care while they were gone. Stan didn't hear any of it as he scooped up Cade and the two of them got busy playing farm with Cade's tractors and toy farm animals.

Beth shooed Tom and Anne out the door and started doing what she loved to do most: nurture her family. The baby was sleeping and Stan was busy with Cade, so Beth started a load of laundry, put a roast in the oven, and started vacuuming.

Tom went into the examination room with Anne. After discussing the symptoms Anne was experiencing and doing some blood work, Dr. Benton prescribed a mild antidepressant medication for Anne. He also suggested that Tom arrange for some extra help for Anne over the next several weeks. Initially, Anne started to object, but her reasons were weak. She admitted that extra help for the next few weeks would be nice, at least until she started feeling a little better.

On the way home, Anne and Tom talked about the kind of help she would like. Anne agreed to allow Karen and Beth to help out, but she didn't want anyone else involved. Tom thought about it and agreed that between him, his mom, and Karen, they could arrange a workable schedule. For the next month, Beth came over and stayed with Anne and the boys from 8:00 a.m. until noon. Karen came over from 1:00 p.m. until 5:00 p.m., and Tom made sure he was home by 6:00 each evening. Beth made meals for the day and cleaned the house. She also made sure Anne got up and showered each morning. Anne tended to the children and took naps as needed. She was very appreciative of the help and Beth's positive attitude.

Karen started the laundry when she arrived and did the dishes from lunch. Then she and Anne read and discussed scripture. She also tended to the boys when Anne took a nap. Karen started dinner so it would be ready when Tom got home. She also ended each visit with prayer. That generally left Anne feeling encouraged and loved.

Tom was so grateful for his mom and Karen. They both stepped up to help Anne and were very uplifting. He could sense that Anne was improving with each passing week. Having the house in order, meals prepared, and an extra hand with the boys gave Anne the time and assurance she needed to get rest and start to feel better. Tom's duties included feeding the boys and getting them ready for bed with baths and extra snuggles. He also made sure to enjoy conversation with Anne.

By the end of the first month, Anne was already feeling better. She had increased energy and was taking better care of herself. She stopped nursing the baby because of the potential harm the anti-depressants might pose to Clay. Anne felt good about the decision because she knew getting better was the most important thing she could do for Clay. He was content with the bottle and was well nourished.

During the second month of Anne's recovery, Beth and Karen cut back their time with Anne, helping out once a day from 10:00 a.m. to 2:00 p.m. Anne began to take on more responsibilities and stopped needing to take naps. She spent more time caring for the boys and playing with them. On the days Karen came over, they were still reading scripture together.

Anne took over all her former duties and full-time care of the boys at the beginning of the third month. She and Karen started doing their scripture reading over the phone while the boys took their naps. Tom called frequently to talk with Anne and make sure she was okay. Occasionally, Beth sent a meal home with Tom for the family to share.

Tom remembered how much Anne loved to hike and find secret little gardens. He called Jeff, Karen's husband, for some help with his plan to create a special place for Anne to enjoy. Prior to going into seminary, Jeff had worked for a landscaper, and Tom was sure he could give him some valuable tips. Together, the two of them created a special garden for Anne.

By the time Clay was six and a half months old, the garden was ready for its unveiling. Anne and Karen had been praying continually for Anne's healing from depression. When Anne felt she was ready, she talked with the doctor about discontinuing the medication. He agreed to decrease her medication with the goal of Anne getting completely off it. That was a huge victory for Anne.

"Honey, Mom and Dad are here. They are going to watch the boys for a couple of hours. There is something I want to show you," Tom said with a big smile.

"Thomas Williams, I know that smile! What are you up to?" Anne insisted.

The sun was just starting to dip beneath the trees as they set out toward the hiking path. With perfect timing, thousands of white twinkling lights Tom and Jeff had hung illuminated the path. It was absolutely magical. Tom and Anne walked hand in hand to the clearing. Once there, they walked under the trellis toward the freshly painted white glider. The pink roses had just started climbing the trellis. On either side of the glider were two small wrought iron tables with lanterns glowing. One table had a bottle of champagne on ice with two champagne glasses. On the other table was a chilled container of smoked salmon and crackers. Tom led Anne to the glider. She slowly sat down, allowing herself to take in every second of the moment. Gradually her eyes turned to the birch tree, and there was the sign Tom had painted and hung on the tree.

Anne reached over and kissed Tom and said, "You have taken my breath away. I have never seen anything so amazingly beautiful and romantic. Thank you for all of this, Tom. It is so lovely. But why? It isn't my birthday or a holiday."

"I wanted to do something special for you. I wanted you to have a special place to go when you want to get away and relax. I also wanted you to have a reminder that you came out of a huge battle and won. There isn't anything we can't do as long as we are together. I am so very proud of you, Anne. This is one small way I can show you how very much you mean to me and the boys. I love you, sweetheart."

They spent hours that evening talking, laughing, planning for the future, and praying prayers of gratitude.

CHAPTER 11

Anne sighed with mixed emotion as she recalled that very difficult time in her life. She noticed Karen's coffee cup was empty and said, "I'm going to refill our coffee cups. I'll be right back."

When Anne returned with the coffee, Karen reminded her, "You were not at the top of your game during that time in your life, but no one is on top all the time. The important thing is that you allowed us into your life and gave yourself a chance at recovery."

"I know, you're right. It was hard for me to be on the receiving end of so much kindness, prayer, service, and love. It was also a time when I know the Lord carried me through each day. He does that every day, but during that time in my life, my thoughts were so dark that I know without him I wouldn't have made it," Anne admitted.

"Are you ready to continue our hike?" Karen asked, ready to change the subject.

"I sure am!"

They continued on down the meandering trail, crossing over a lively, clear stream on an old swinging footbridge. The water trickled over shiny, slick rocks on its way down to the pond. The frogs, crickets, and nightingales made their own music along the way.

"Anne, when the boys were old enough for Sunday school, who talked Jeff into a Sunday school program at the church?" Karen asked knowing full well the answer.

"It was me, and you know it." Anne smiled. "We had AWANA, which is great, but no Sunday school program. My boys were going to have Sunday school!"

Karen added, "If I remember right, you and Jeff went toe to toe on that one."

Anne had talked with Jeff several times about starting a Sunday school program at the church they attended where Jeff was the pastor. Jeff was very satisfied with the AWANA program that had been running for years at the church. He believed that a Sunday school program would require more volunteer teachers than he could convince to participate. He didn't think there was room for both programs in their small church.

Anne had fond memories of attending Sunday school and Vacation Bible School. It was the sweet memories of learning about Jesus with other children and doing activities that brought the stories to life that Anne insisted be part of her sons' lives. With that in mind, Anne knocked on Jeff's office door.

"Come in," Jeff cheerfully instructed whoever had just knocked on his door. He could tell by the look on Anne's face that he was about to hear yet another plea for Sunday school.

"Good morning, Jeff! I'm going to guess that you probably already know what I am going to talk to you about today," Anne suggested in a friendly, yet determined manner.

"I suppose I do. Come on in and sit down. Let's talk Sunday school."

"Thanks, Jeff. I know I sound like a broken record, but this is really near and dear to my heart. So much so that I have drawn up a plan to incorporate a Sunday school program into our church without affecting AWANA. I believe this will get more of the families and other adults involved in the church and have a positive influence on the children's lives."

"Okay, you have my attention. Let's hear your plan. Hey, before we get started, can I offer you a cup of coffee?"

Anne, anxious to roll out her plan, said, "No thanks, but you go ahead if you would like some."

"I think I will," Jeff said as he grabbed his coffee mug and filled it full with the piping-hot Jamaican blend that he loved.

Anne started, "I think we should start the program with kindergarten through sixth grade. We have roughly five children per grade who would attend. We could set up partitions in the fellowship hall to delineate classrooms. We would need 14 teachers, two per class. By using two teachers per class, if one had another obligation one Sunday, we would have a backup. If we hold Sunday school during the 9:15 a.m. service, the parents can drop off their children at Sunday school and head upstairs for worship. It also offers them a chance to drop off the children, attend Bible study, pick them up, and then attend the second church service together as a whole family. I have four curriculums we could consider for the program. All of them are highly rated. I think you will find that one of them stands out a little more than the rest for its level of comprehension and fun activities."

"Well, you have really given this some thought. Have you also thought about where 14 volunteers are going to come from?" Jeff asked.

"I have thought about it. I want to present the idea at both church services next week and see how many people I can get to volunteer."

"Okay, Anne, you can present your idea in both services, but if you don't have at least 14 volunteers by the following Sunday, we are done talking about it, and there won't be Sunday school."

Jeff was reluctant to allow Anne to pursue the topic any further, but if she could get the volunteers and the congregation would support it, why not?

The next Sunday, Anne came prepared to inspire the congregation and 14 adult volunteers to support Sunday school in their church. Jeff finished his sermon and announced to the congregation that Anne wanted to propose the idea of instituting Sunday school in their church for children in kindergarten through sixth grade.

"Come on up, Anne, and share your plan with the congregation."

Anne had never been much for public speaking, but the Lord had laid this idea on her heart, and she simply couldn't let it go. With notes in hand, Anne walked up to the pulpit and began to share her plan.

"Good morning, everyone! Thank you, Pastor Jeff, for giving me this opportunity to speak with the congregation. By a show of hands, how many of you have attended a Sunday school? Wow, it looks like almost all of you have! Now, by a show of hands, how many of you have fond memories of attending Sunday school? The same number of hands went up again. Great! What are some of those precious memories?" Anne asked.

It started out slowly, but gradually, people started to respond.

Susan Gentry said, "I loved learning about Jesus through stories."

"Singing the hymns with other kids was fun," Kathy Brown added.

Brian White said, "I loved the snacks! Mrs. Williams makes a mean chocolate chip cookie."

"The Christmas program was always one of my favorite memories," said Mrs. Fellows, the pianist.

Suddenly, vivid memories of having fun, learning about Jesus, and growing up together as a church family were being shared throughout the entire congregation. Eventually, Anne reined in the conversation.

"All the things you have mentioned are exactly why I believe having a Sunday school program is so vital to our children. They need to have the same sense of community and love we all experienced growing up in the church with Sunday school."

Everyone seemed to be in agreement, so Anne posed her request for teacher teams.

"Let's make this happen, and in order to take the first steps, we will need 14 adult volunteer teachers. This will be an amazing experience for both the adults and the children. Imagine being able to help develop these young children to become strong in their faith, equipping them with the lessons they need to ward off the negative forces of this world. We have almost all attended Sunday school, so you know it does not require a degree in teaching, only an honest desire to serve these little lambs. You will be paired in twos to teach each class; that way, if someone can't make it, we have a backup, and the children's learning doesn't need to be disrupted. Please pray about volunteering and let me know by the end of the week which grade level you would like to share Jesus with. I will also be in the lobby after this service to answer any questions you might have and register you as a teacher. Thank you for considering this and for the trip down memory lane!"

Anne returned to her seat and let out a huge sigh of relief. She said a silent prayer to God, asking him to stir the hearts of the congregation. Anne repeated her plea for volunteers to run a Sunday school program at the next service. After each service, she stood behind the information desk answering questions and registering teachers. After the parishioners left the second service, she added up the number of volunteers. Thirty-one members had answered the call to teach Sunday school. Five people asked her for a list of supplies she would need so they could donate the items.

Anne took the information to Jeff as he and Karen sat in his office waiting for the outcome.

Karen gave Anne a big hug and said, "Great job! I loved how you got the entire congregation involved!"

Jeff concurred, "You did a great job and gave it your all, but I'm sure you didn't come up with the numbers you needed. To be fair, I will give you to the end of the week to try."

Anne smiled and handed the sign-up sheet to Jeff. "Well, if we have any more volunteers, I'm not sure what I'll do with them."

Jeff looked up from the paperwork, somewhat dumbfounded, and said, "Congratulations! You have yourself a Sunday school program. I guess I need to look at the curriculums you gave me more closely. Let's meet again on Wednesday to iron out more of the details. Good job, Anne!"

PART 2
Rachel's Forgiveness

Bear with each other and forgive one another
if any of you has a grievance against someone.
Forgive as the Lord forgave you.

—Col. 3:13

CHAPTER 12

"It was really amazing to see God's hand at work on that Sunday school project back then," Anne commented to Karen.

"It sure was! Look at how it has grown. We now have, on average, 50 children in each grade level, so the classes are divided in half. Hundreds of children have come to know Jesus through your steadfast determination to obey the Lord's prompting to you."

Karen gave her friend a squeeze and said, "This has been great, Anne. It's time I head back home to make supper for Jeff. Let's talk some more tomorrow. Why don't you stop by my place tomorrow morning around 9:00 so we can pick up where we left off?"

"You are the best friend I have ever had, Karen. Are you sure you want to continue this trip down memory lane?" Anne asked, secretly praying that Karen would be up for day two.

"Of course! Let's plan on having lunch at that cute little coffee shop that just opened. What's the name? I remember, it's called Perk Place. I have heard great things about their lunches."

"It's a date," Anne said cheerfully.

The two friends started their walk back to Anne's house. They chatted about local events coming up in their community. There was going to be a book reading at the library Monday night. The author was going to be doing the reading himself. The biannual Women's Conference was being hosted at their church. Karen was busy making arrangements for the speakers. She had long since closed the registration and was expecting 150 women, twice as many as they had ever had in attendance.

Eventually, Karen and Anne made it back to Anne's house. They prayed together, thanking their Lord and Savior for his presence in their conversations. Karen gave Anne a hug and said, "I'll see you tomorrow, my friend."

"You will. Nine a.m. sharp!"

As Karen was driving out, Tom was pulling into the driveway. He had always been grateful for the friendship Karen and Anne shared. The two of them had been there for each other through good times and bad. He knew that when there was something going on with Anne that he didn't understand, Karen would understand.

Tom stepped out of his pickup, his dented and well-worn lunch box in hand, grabbed his wife, and gave her a big kiss.

"Wow, welcome home, Tom!"

"How's my beautiful bride?" Tom asked, truly wanting to know if she was feeling any better.

"I am starting to feel a little better. Karen and I had a great talk today. She helped open my eyes to some of the kingdom work I have been involved in. We are going to get together tomorrow at Karen's house to talk some more. I guess I feel hopeful that by talking things out, I will have some answers to the questions I have. You, my dear, have been so supportive and loving! Thank you for being patient, too."

"Mom sent over supper for us."

"She is so sweet, but she really didn't need to do that," Anne stated.

"Well, we are in luck tonight, because she made too much for supper and asked me to take some of the food off her hands. She hasn't been able to successfully reduce the amount of food she prepares. I swear, she cooks for 20 people for each meal," Tom said with sincerity.

"So, you didn't tell her I am struggling?" Anne asked suspiciously.

"No, I didn't. It's not up to me to share that. I think that's a private matter, and if you choose to tell her, it's up to you."

"Thank you, Tom. Let's not let that supper get cold. I love your mom's fried chicken!"

Tom smiled and said, "That's my girl!"

Tom and Anne enjoyed the tasty meal prepared for them. After doing the dishes, Tom opened a bottle of wine, and the two of them sat down in the Adirondack chairs in front of the fire Tom had started in their outdoor fireplace.

"Anne, I checked with both of the boys, and they will be here Sunday with their families."

"Thanks for reminding them, honey. I need some family time. There is nothing like having those sweet little grandbabies wrap their chubby little arms around my neck and give me kisses," Anne said, sighing at the thought.

"Our little Mavis is such a sweet little hugger. I have to admit she has me wrapped around her tiny little finger. When Cade wiggles her out of her car seat and she runs to me with her arms reaching up, saying, 'Poppa, Poppa, up,' my heart melts."

"Then we have Clay and Jessica's little angel, Lucy," Anne added. She has had hold of my heart from the day she was born. Her big sparkling blue eyes, sweet little baby smile, and soft blond curls fill me with joy. It will be impossible for me to say no to that little one. She is so alert for a three-month-old. She doesn't miss a thing."

"I never could have imagined what joy I could feel from being a grandfather to two little girls," Tom admitted.

"Tom, we really have been blessed. We raised two healthy and reasonably happy boys and launched them. Cade and Clay both have a strong relationship with Jesus Christ. They both seem very happy in their marriages, and they are both terrific fathers.

"Tom, I think that having Christ in the center of our marriage has made all the difference. Hopefully, our marriage and your parents' marriage have been good examples for the boys to follow. Lots of other couples that married within a few years of us have been divorced, remarried, and divorced again. As I think about those couples, they didn't have Jesus Christ in the center of their lives or marriages. I am so grateful that we have been able to grow individually and together in Christ."

"Anne, you must be feeling a little bit better. I can hear it in your voice and in the positive outlook you have tonight. It must have helped to talk with Karen today," Tom suggested.

"Actually, I do feel a little better. Karen reminded me of the times when the Lord has used me to advance his kingdom. It's easy to overlook those times that happened so long ago, but they did happen. Thank you, Tom, for being so patient with me."

"I didn't do much, but you're welcome!"

Tom added another log to the fire and slid his chair next to Anne's. No sooner had he sat down that they saw headlights shining up their driveway. The truck came to a screeching halt and out jumped Cade with a sleepy little Mavis in his arms. Tom motioned to Cade to come around back.

As soon as Cade got close enough to Tom and Anne, they both knew something was very wrong. Cade handed Mavis to Anne and sat down across from Tom and Anne.

With a shaky voice, Cade said, "I don't really know what happened, but Rachel is gone. I still can't quite get my head around all of this. She left both of us. Why would she do that? Until I got home tonight and found the note and her things gone, I would never have thought that anything was wrong. We have a two-year-old daughter and a whole future together. I have no idea why she would want to throw all of that away. I have tried to call her over and over, but the calls always go to voicemail. I've tried texting, too."

"Cade, have you talked with Clay or Jessica? Anne asked. They may have heard from Rachel."

"I called Clay as soon as I found the note. Neither of them has heard from Rachel in days. That's odd, too," Cade stated. "Clay and Jessica are making calls to everyone they can think of to try to find Rachel. Clay said to let him know if I want him to drive around and look. Jessica said that Rachel has been distant lately. They used to talk on the phone a couple times a week. Jessica said the last time she saw Rachel was about six weeks ago when she dropped off some baby clothes for Lucy."

"Cade, there are a lot of missing pieces. We will sort it all out, but it may not happen as quickly as you would like. Before jumping to any conclusions, let's pray and ask God to guide us through all of this," Tom suggested.

Tom prayed for Cade, Rachel, and Mavis. He asked that the Lord guide them in helping to bring the family back together again. Afterward, Anne took Mavis inside to lay her down in the crib they had set up for the occasional sleepovers they hosted for their granddaughters.

Anne changed Mavis and got her ready for bed. She took the often-read *The Poky Little Puppy* Little Golden Book off the shelf to read to Mavis as she rocked her to sleep. It was the same book she read many years ago to both her boys when they were infants. Once Mavis was asleep, Anne gently laid her in the crib and joined Tom and Cade.

They had poured over the note Rachel had left for Cade. There really weren't any clues as to what had happened, other than she left. Anne called Rachel on her cell phone and left a message, saying, "Rachel, please call me to let me know you are safe. Whatever has happened, we can work things out. Please come home, and we can talk things through. Cade and Mavis love you and need you. Tom and I love you, too. I am praying for your safety and that you come back home."

"Anne, Cade and I are going to drive around for a while and see if we can find her," Tom said. "If you hear from Rachel, let us know, and we will call you if we have any luck locating her."

Cade asked, "Do you think we should call the police?"

"They really can't do anything. She is an adult and has the legal right to leave. Let's get going and start looking," Tom said, feeling very uncomfortable just sitting around talking and not taking any action.

About 45 minutes after Tom and Cade left, another set of lights came up the driveway. This time it was Rachel's car. Anne went to the door and opened it to find Rachel standing there. Her eyes were swollen from crying. Anne reached out to her and gave her a hug just as she started to sob.

"Come inside, dear. I have been asking God to lead you back home, and here you are. I have a pot of tea brewing. Let's sit down and begin to unravel what happened."

Rachel sighed, "Oh, Anne, you are so kind, and I don't deserve your kindness. I have really messed up. I don't know if any of this can be repaired. I have been a fool. I did get your message, and it brought me to my senses. You have always been very supportive of me, and I knew I could come here to talk with you."

"Rachel, you are always welcome here. I do need to call Tom and let him and Cade know you are here. I'll need to call Clay and Jessica, too. We have all been worried sick."

"Anne, I doubt Cade wants to see me after what I did," Rachel said with resignation.

"Believe me, Rachel, Cade does want to see you. Tell me, what happened? None of this makes sense. By the way, Mavis is sleeping soundly in the guest room."

Between sobs, Rachel shared with Anne everything that had happened. "This is really hard to admit, especially to my mother-in-law, but I may as well be honest. It started about three months ago. I met a man at the playgroup I take Mavis to. He is a stay-at-home dad, and we started commiserating with each other. That led to playdates with our children. He suggested that we meet at a park out of town so no one would assume we were doing anything wrong. It was kind of exciting to think that another man might be interested in me. Cade has been working long hours, and well, I came up with lots of excuses for my behavior."

Rachel continued, "The relationship grew more serious, and he would call me late at night after Cade was asleep. I justified it to myself by saying it was harmless and Cade was sleeping anyway. I know this is really bad, but I am going to continue. We had conversations daily and playdates at least three times a week. Two days ago, he confessed his love for me and talked about the wonderful life we were going to have together. We could leave it all behind and have a fresh start. I asked Cade to pick up Mavis from my mom's, and I packed and left. He left his family behind and picked me up. We were gone for about two hours when the reality of everything I had done came crashing in on me. I was leaving behind everyone I love for some romantic notion of a relationship. I had been ignoring Cade's calls and texts. Something inside me told me to listen to your voice message. It was what I needed to hear to wake me up to the huge mistake I was making. I insisted he bring me home. I pray you can forgive me, Anne. I don't deserve Cade's forgiveness, but I pray he will find it in his heart to forgive me and give me another chance."

Anne said a silent prayer before responding to Rachel, asking the Holy Spirit to guide her words and grant her wisdom to handle the situation and Rachel wisely.

"Rachel, do you see how you let Satan in your life? He is the king of lies and deception. What happened started slowly and innocently enough. You need to understand that Satan loves nothing more than to break families apart, and he will use any method possible to do that. We begin to believe the lies he feeds us, and once on that slippery slope, it doesn't take long to fall. It is our duty as wives to pray for our husbands and our marriages all the time. They need protection—divine protection—at all times. You will need to be completely honest with Cade so you can begin to heal your precious marriage. That little girl in the other room deserves to have both her mommy and daddy in her life."

"I can't believe I thought she would be better off without me. It's true, I bought into a huge sack of lies. I hope my baby can forgive me." Rachel was sobbing again. Just then, Tom and Cade pulled into the driveway. Cade jumped out of the truck and ran into the house. He opened the kitchen door and found Rachel and his mom sitting at the table. Rachel's eyes were swollen from what seemed like hours of crying. Tom walked in and stopped, taking in all of what was going on in his home.

Cade reached for Rachel and said, "I'm so glad you're okay and home."

Rachel pulled back slightly and said, "It's good to see you, Cade, but you may not be as relieved to see me once I tell you what has been going on with me. I hope you can hear me out before you react."

Anne recommended they go home together to talk in private and leave Mavis with them for the night. Cade felt his stomach leap to his throat, and his heart started to pound. He knew his mom would not be suggesting a private talk unless the news was bad. They agreed to Anne's suggestion. Cade told his parents he would be over to pick up Mavis by 8:00 the next morning. Cade and Rachel rode home together in Cade's truck.

"What in the hell happened?" Tom demanded. "Cade was about out of his mind looking for her. How could she just pick up and leave Cade and Mavis like that?"

"Honestly, Rachel let Satan in and began believing his lies. Thankfully, I think she is starting to understand how she nearly threw away her marriage and her precious child. We have to pray for them. It is going to be a very rough night for our son. At least Rachel has started to process what happened. Hopefully, their marriage can withstand this trial."

Anne then shared the whole story with Tom. She knew that Cade would need to talk with his dad about all of this tomorrow. Tom was grateful that Rachel had come to her senses, but he wasn't so sure Cade would be able to forgive her. They were going to need a lot of support.

CHAPTER 13

"Mommy! MOMMY! I ready to get up now," Mavis called out.

Neither Tom nor Anne slept very well that night. Anne sat up in bed and rubbed the sleep out of her eyes. She heard her granddaughter's call for her mommy and got up to get her out of bed.

"Mommy! Mommy! MOMMY!" Mavis demanded.

"Good morning, my little sunshine! Mommy isn't here right now. You are stuck with me and Grandpa!" Anne said a quick prayer, thanking the Lord that Rachel was at least home with family and not off with someone else.

"Poppa! Poppa!" Mavis squealed.

Mavis, Tom's first grandchild, had this big, rough-and-tumble farmer wrapped around her little finger. Never having had a sister or a daughter, Tom felt very blessed to have Mavis.

"Where's my Mavis?" Tom asked as he walked into the room, pretending he couldn't see her. He looked behind the curtains, under the crib, and in the closet. All the while, Mavis was giggling and saying, "I here, Poppa, I here!"

Tom reached over Anne, lifted Mavis out of her arms, and then tossed her into the air. "You seem a little light! I think we need to get you some pancakes, little miss! What do you say we talk Grandma into wrestling us up a few pancakes and some sausage?" Tom suggested to Mavis.

Tom put Mavis on the floor, and she began to dance around Anne, singing, "Pan-a-cakes, pan-a-cakes, we want pan-a-cakes!" Tom joined in on the fun. Anne shook her head, leaving the two of them to sing and dance while she whipped up some "pan-a-cakes." The first order of business in the kitchen, however, was to start a pot of coffee.

Anne heard the familiar sound of Tom's cell phone ringing. Tom picked up the call.

"Good morning, son. How's it going?"

"Dad, I don't know what is going to happen between Rachel and me. If it's okay with you, I need to take the day off. We still have a lot to work through. Do you think you and Mom can keep Mavis another day? Cade asked. I can run over with some clothes and Pull-Ups."

"Of course, Cade, we can take care of Mavis. In fact, I'm going to take off today, too. It will be nice for us and Mavis to have a little bonding time, as your mom puts it. Are you two taking care of yourselves?"

"I don't know, Dad. How do you pick up the pieces after something like this? It's embarrassing, and I am really angry with her," Cade admitted.

"If I could make a suggestion, why don't you call Pastor Jeff? I bet if you call him now, he would make time to see both of you today."

"I don't know. A pastor? What's he going to do?" Cade asked, reluctant to air their personal business to the pastor they see every Sunday.

"Son, the devil just weaseled his way into your marriage. It is going to take a lot more than just the two of you talking it out together. It's a great start, but let's increase the odds of working this through successfully by bringing in Pastor Jeff. He knows a thing or two about broken relationships and how to mend them. It will be okay. What the two of you discuss with him goes no further than his office."

Cade said, "All right, Dad, you are probably right. I'll make sure Rachel is willing to talk with Pastor Jeff and then make the call."

"I love you, son."

"I love you, too, Dad. And thanks for being there for Mavis, Rachel, and me. It means a lot," Cade said sincerely.

After the call, Tom scooped up his pride and joy and headed into the kitchen. Anne had poured Tom's coffee and set it on the counter. The hearty smells of a country breakfast filled the air. Sausage was frying in the pan, and Mavis's "pan-a-cakes" were cooking on the griddle. Tom slid Mavis into her high chair and poured orange juice into her favorite Elsa and Anna sippy cup.

Tom asked Anne, "Did you hear any of that conversation? Cade called and needs some more time. He asked if we would take care of Mavis today. I know you have plans with Karen, so I took the day off, too. It's one of the perks of being the boss," Tom added, trying to lighten the mood a little.

"I did hear bits and pieces. How do you think Cade is holding up?"

"He isn't letting on, but it's clear he is torn up about it. I suggested they call Pastor Jeff and talk openly with him."

Anne commented, "Cade is a very private person. I hope he follows through."

"I think he will. By the way, he will be over here soon with some things for our little princess. I don't know if Rachel will come along, but my guess is it will just be Cade."

"I think I should cancel with Karen and stay back to help you with her," Anne said, lightly touching her finger to Mavis's nose.

"Anne, I appreciate it, but I can take care of this little buckaroo. In fact, I may take her over to see Great-Grandpa and Great-Grandma," Tom suggested.

"I know Stan and Beth would love to see her. Okay, but you call me if you need anything at all or if things change and Cade needs me," Anne insisted.

"I will, but we do have to remember that we are simply in a supportive role now. That's part of having adult children. Cade and Rachel are going to have some difficult decisions to make, and all we can do is stand on the sidelines and pray that they make good ones."

Just then Cade drove up the driveway. Rachel was in the truck but did not come in. Cade had packed a diaper bag full of all the things Mavis would need and then some. He looked haggard and thanked them for taking care of Mavis. Before leaving, Cade told his parents that he and Rachel were on their way to see Pastor Jeff. He promised to keep them updated.

CHAPTER 14

Jeff was awakened by an early morning phone call. It was Cade Williams asking Jeff to meet with him and Rachel. Jeff could tell by Cade's voice and his willingness to reach out that it had to be something serious. He quickly agreed to meet them at his office in an hour.

"Karen, honey, I have to leave early for the office. Do you think you could make me some breakfast while I shower?" Jeff asked. He really hoped she would be willing to get breakfast going. He could tell by the phone call that he would need to be on top of his game, and he always thought more clearly after he had something to eat.

"What? Breakfast? Okay. Hmm, how does oatmeal with strawberries and cream sound?" Karen asked, still half-asleep.

"That sounds fantastic! Thank you, honey. You have no idea how much that is going to help me and the couple I am meeting," Jeff said, always grateful for Karen's ability to be flexible with the demands of pastoring a church.

Freshly showered and dressed, Jeff came into the kitchen to find his breakfast prepared exactly the way he liked it. Karen and Jeff prayed, thanking the Lord for their meal, and asked him to direct their thoughts, words, and actions throughout the day. As soon as they finished eating, Jeff filled his travel mug with coffee, kissed his wife, and headed out the door.

As Karen was straightening up the kitchen, she was thankful for a husband who loved her sincerely and loved the people of their congregation. Once her morning chores were done, she sat down in her favorite reading chair in the den and started her scripture reading. She established a routine of praying for insight, reading scripture, and then working on her Bible study.

Karen was suddenly pulled from her Bible study with a light knock on the door. She looked up at the clock and remembered Anne was coming over.

Yikes! I haven't even gotten dressed yet! Karen said to herself. She pulled on her robe and went to the door.

"My goodness! Did you forget I was coming over, or are we having a pajama party and I forgot about the dress code?" Anne asked with a giggle.

Karen grabbed Anne's arm and pulled her into the house, laughing. "Let's not let any vicious rumors get started about the pastor's wife not getting dressed in the morning."

Karen explained, "Jeff got a call early this morning to meet with a couple from church. I got up with him so we could have breakfast together. We finished, and I jumped into my devotions and, well, kind of let time slip away, and here we are! Help yourself to some coffee, and I'll get dressed."

While Karen was getting dressed, Anne checked her phone for messages. She did have one message from Tom. It was a picture of Stan and Beth reading to Mavis and then another picture of Mavis jumping in piles of leaves. *Tom is an amazing husband, father, and grandpa. How many men actually take the time to take pictures of their granddaughter and send them to their wives?* Anne thought.

Soon Karen was dressed and ready to spend time with her friend. Karen looked over at Anne with the phone in her hand and asked, "Is everything okay? You seem a million miles away."

"I guess I am. I was just thinking how blessed I am to have Tom as my hubby. He just sent me some pictures he took of Mavis and of Mavis with his parents."

"Mavis is getting a little special time with her poppa today?" Karen asked.

"She spent the night last night, and Cade asked if we could keep her today so he and Rachel could have some time to themselves. I'm afraid they are going through a serious rough spot right now," Anne added.

"Is there anything I can do or maybe anything Jeff can help them with?" Karen asked out of concern for both Cade and Rachel.

"Actually, they are with Jeff right now. Hopefully, he can help guide them in a more positive direction. Keep them in your prayers."

Karen suggested they head out early to Perk Place. She needed to make a stop at the quilt shop before they stopped for coffee. The quilt shop just got in a new shipment of material. Karen had special ordered some fabric to use for decorating the venue for the Women's Conference and wanted to see if it had come in.

On the way there, Karen said, "We never finished talking about your concerns yesterday. Let's pick up where we left off."

"Gosh, with everything going on, I forgot where we left off," Anne admitted.

"Well, we were going over some of the kingdom work you have been involved in, and when I went home last night, we had just talked about getting the Sunday school program going, against all odds—namely my husband." Karen smiled.

"That was so good for the boys and all the other children in the congregation."

"Anne, it was great for everyone! Think about all the people who got involved who otherwise never would have if you hadn't been persistent. You were courageous and obeyed God's desire for you," Karen said.

"Here we are," Karen added. "Come on in and check out the quilt shop. They have some beautiful quilts on display. Women from all over bring in quilts they made from kits purchased at the store. The owner displays them and sells more kits. When women bring their completed quilts in, they get 10 percent off their next purchase. I think it's really a smart business idea."

Beautiful shades of colorful fabric were stacked neatly on display racks. One section had the warm and fuzzy flannels in burgundy, pumpkin, harvest gold, and olive green. Another section was chock-full of baby-nursery-type fabrics. Anne's eye was drawn to the back corner where soft pastel flowers and gentle shades of yellow and pink designs were prominent. There was a sweet country-type quilt draped over an old rocking chair. Above the chair hung a sign that said, "Little Grandma's Corner."

Winkie, the store owner, came to the counter to talk with Karen. She had Karen's order in her hand. Curious, Anne asked, "Why is that fabric in the back corner called Little Grandma's Corner?

"It's in honor of my grandmother. When my brothers and I were young, we grew up calling our mom's mom Little Grandma, and it stuck. She was an amazing woman who was quiet, yet strong. She was always serving others. The fabrics displayed are similar to the fabric of her era and the type of fabric she wore. We all loved her and miss her. I guess it's my small way of acknowledging her even now. Thank you for asking."

"I have your order here, Karen. Let me know if there is anything else you need. I am available to come and help decorate if you want an extra hand," Winkie offered.

Karen said, "Absolutely! The more the merrier!" Karen paid for the fabric, and they left for the coffee shop.

Perk Place, although new in town, was decorated with a rustic country sort of flair. The walls were covered in weathered barn board. A corrugated metal welcome sign was displayed just as you walked through the door. Anne spotted a cozy circular booth in the back near the huge fieldstone fireplace. The warm flames danced and crackled, warming everyone seated nearby.

"Isn't this place just the best?" Karen claimed.

"It has a homey feel, like it has been here all along. This place even smells amazing! Someone has been baking pies long before we got here," Anne said as she slid into the booth and looked around.

Within a few minutes, the sweet young waitress stopped by their table to take their order.

Anne looked up from the menu and asked the waitress, "Is that fresh pecan pie in the bakery case I saw when we came in?"

"It sure is! My mom baked it early this morning. Can I get you a piece of pie?"

"I know I probably shouldn't, but what the heck! Yes, I would like a slice of that wonderful pecan pie with a scoop of ice cream and a cup of regular coffee."

"You got it," the waitress said with a smile and then turned to Karen. "How about you, ma'am? What can I get you on this beautiful autumn day?"

"Well, if you are going all in, Anne, so am I! I'll have a slice of pumpkin pie with a dollop of whip cream on the side and a cup of regular coffee."

"Okay, ladies, I'll be right back with your order." With that, the young woman made her way back to the kitchen.

Karen turned to Anne, "You are becoming a bad influence on me! Don't tell Jeff I had pie this morning. I've been after him to cut back on sweets."

"We could cancel our orders if you're concerned—you know, about Jeff," Anne teased.

"Not a chance!"

Switching topics, Karen shared, "You will never guess who I saw the other day at the library. I had just dropped off my books at the counter, and who was standing behind me but Clay's old teacher Mrs. Witt. I had to bite my tongue. Having a sore tongue from biting down on it is one of the hazards of being the wife of a pastor. After everything Clay went through with her that year, not to mention the fight you and Tom had to go through with her and the school board. She must be back in town or she wouldn't have been at the library returning her books."

"I have to admit, I hope I don't cross paths with her anytime soon. I shudder to think how she bullied Clay, and he just took it for the longest time. In fact, it wasn't until a friend of Clay's mentioned it to Cade that any of us even knew about it. Clay always had fun at school and was a decent student until the 10th grade and Mrs. Witt's English class. There was something about Clay that she simply didn't like, and she went out of her way to embarrass him daily in class. Clay became more and more withdrawn until we really had a hard time getting him to go to school," Anne remembered with pangs of regret that she didn't realize what was happening sooner.

Karen said, "What was really strange was that she seemed totally unaware of how she was affecting Clay and the other students in that class."

"That's right. When we went to the principal, he couldn't believe that what was reported to us was true because there hadn't been any other complaints from parents. Honestly, Clay's classmates were well aware of what was going on. I'm sure they didn't want to say anything for fear of becoming her next target."

"I think the turning point for Clay was when you and Tom had that family meeting and talked the whole thing through. Clay had been bullied by her for so long that he was beginning to believe the lies she was saying about him. Once he saw that all of you were in his corner, he began to come around again," Karen commented.

"Yes, but we still had some work to do. We weren't going to get her to stop until the principal could truly see what was going on. I am so grateful that the kids who let Cade in on the trouble with Mrs. Witt were willing to talk with their parents and come to a meeting prior to our conference with the principal."

CHAPTER 15

It was nearly 7:00 p.m., the time Tom and Anne had set to meet with the parents and the kids who had reported Mrs. Witt's behavior toward Clay. Cade and Clay were shooting baskets in the driveway when four cars pulled in. It was Jessica Reacher and her parents, Scott and Naomi. Travis Deal and his parents, Richard and Stacie, were also there. And then there were Jeremy Forrester and his father, Justin, and Kaitlyn Robinson and her parents, Dan and Faith. The boys greeted their guests and led them into the house. Anne and Tom said a quick prayer as soon as they saw the cars approaching. First, they thanked God that the families showed up, and second, they asked God to be present in the meeting and that his will be done.

Once everyone was seated, Tom started the meeting by thanking everyone for coming and for taking the matter seriously.

Justin Forrester spoke up right away, shaking Clay's hand, saying, "I'm sorry this has happened to you, Clay. You don't deserve it, and I'm glad we are all here to do something about it. If it can happen to you, it can happen to any of the students."

Anne stood next to Tom and said, "We wouldn't have called you all here if our own efforts to address this had worked. Unfortunately, the principal said that to address the issue with Mrs. Witt, he needs more evidence that what we reported took place. It's our hope that we can all come together Thursday night at the school board meeting to address the issue with both the principal and the members of the school board. If you are willing to share on Thursday night, I will get us on the agenda for the meeting."

With a unanimous vote of agreement, the families settled back for a night of fun and great conversation. The parents rekindled friendships that had drifted away in the busyness of life. Clay was elated, having regained some of the confidence he had lost months ago.

The next two days of school came and went. Mrs. Witt continued her tirade and bitter resentment toward Clay during class. Unbeknownst to Clay or Mrs. Witt, one of the classmates, Jeremy Forrester, videotaped the class on his cell phone. After school, he shared it with his father. An hour before the school board meeting, Justin shared the video with Tom.

Tom shook his head and said, "Thanks for showing me this, Justin. I hope our presentation at the school board meeting will be enough, but in case it isn't, will you bring the recording? I really hope we don't have to use it. I had no idea she was that bad. Anne will be devastated, and I'm sure it will embarrass Clay."

"If that's how you want it to go, I'm in. Just give me the signal if you want to use it."

"I will. Let's pray it doesn't come to that." But Tom was fairly certain they would have to use it. The school district was far from the big city, and they had trouble getting teachers. In fact, Tom couldn't ever remember hearing about a teacher being let go.

The school board first met in closed session. Then they opened up the meeting to concerned parents, and Tom and Anne were first on the list. They entered the conference room with the Forresters, the Deals, the Reachers, and the Robinsons. Mrs. Witt sat by herself, looking somewhat surprised by the number of people attending for this petty little insignificant complaint made by an entitled farmer's son and his parents.

Tom and Anne told the board what had reluctantly been reported to them by their son Cade concerning his brother. Mrs. Witt sat on her chair, sneering at Clay and thinking to herself, *What's the matter? Little Clay can't take it? Everyone knows this school has a shortage of teachers. They won't get rid of me. They can't. Besides, who is going to believe a conceited teenager over a well-educated teacher?*

The school board president, John Wells, asked Clay if what his parents said was the truth. Before Clay could answer, his friend Jeremy said, "That's not the half of it."

"Okay, son, you'll get your chance to speak. Right now, I'm speaking to Clay." Mr. Wells clarified.

Clay quietly said, "It's true, sir."

One by one, each of Clay's friends and their parents shared additional stories about what had happened to Clay in the classroom.

Then Mr. Wells looked up and asked Mrs. Witt to respond to what the teenagers and their parents had just shared.

Mrs. Witt stood up and responded, "It is simply not true! This bunch of kids hatched a plan to get their parents involved to make me look bad. It is all lies. They and their parents are *liars*! I demand an apology, and Clay needs to be expelled. I have had it!"

"Whoa, whoa, whoa, Mrs. Witt. No one is going to be expelled, and I would appreciate it if you would refrain from calling these devoted parents and their children liars," requested Mr. Wells.

Mr. Wells continued, "We have heard quite a bit of new information tonight. I'm sure we can resolve this quietly. We can see about getting Clay moved to another classroom. Perhaps this is just a personality clash; it happens."

Just then, Dan and Faith Robinson stood up and said, "If Mrs. Witt isn't fired or asked to resign, we are pulling our daughter from the school. How she has damaged Clay this year cannot be tolerated."

Each of the other parents stood up and said the same thing.

"I think we are getting ahead of ourselves. The board should consider everything and come up with a workable solution," Mr. Wells pleaded. "It took the principal three years to find the last teacher we hired."

Tom had tolerated about all he could. He nodded toward Justin and said, "Mr. Wells and members of the board, we do have additional information we would like to share with you, but I ask that the kids be dismissed and that my wife go with them."

"Well, this is highly irregular, but so is everything else that's happened tonight. Go ahead," Mr. Wells instructed.

The kids left the room with Anne. She sat them down in the hallway and prayed with them. At first, the kids felt a little awkward but settled into the prayer. Anne prayed, "Dear Lord God, thank you for this opportunity to be heard in the meeting. Thank you for these teens that have been brave enough to stand up to bullying by a teacher and support Clay. Please be with everyone in the conference room. Help them to see and accept the truth. And Lord, I pray for Mrs. Witt. She is being exposed, and it won't be easy for her. Help her come to you, Lord. May you grant her peace. It is in Jesus's name we pray, Amen."

Jessica asked, "Mrs. Williams, why did you pray for Mrs. Witt? She is a terrible person."

"That may be, but we don't know what is behind her anger. Did you notice that she sat all alone? She doesn't have anyone in her life. If anyone can help her, it will be God," Anne explained.

About 15 minutes later, the doors to the conference room opened, and the teens were allowed back into the room. Mrs. Witt's face was pinched. She took one look at the kids and screamed, "I hope you little brats are happy. I'm through here, finished." She got up and stormed out of the room. Mr. Wells explained what had happened while they were out of the room. The school board watched the last two classes Mrs. Witt taught with Clay. They were appalled and fired her. A report will be made to the state licensing board requesting Mrs. Witt lose her teaching license.

The kids were screaming and jumping up and down, elated that they were heard and that they won. Anne glanced over to Tom and mouthed, "What tape?" Tom smiled and hugged his wife.

Chapter 16

Karen looked over at Anne and said, "If I remember right, you continued to mentor Jessica in her walk with Christ."

"Yes, she is a wonderful young woman. Jessica and her husband, Brad, are leaving for Zimbabwe next month to begin their missionary work there."

"You know, Anne, with everything we talked about yesterday and today, it seems like you have done a fair amount of kingdom work in your 49 years, not to mention raising two amazing young men and being a loving and faithful wife to Tom. Do you still believe that your life hasn't really counted for much?" Karen asked sincerely.

"You have pointed out some critical times in our lives where God did use me to help others. I am grateful that he has called me to serve. It's just that I am left wondering about the rest of my life. My boys don't need me the way they used to. I want my life to mean something significant going forward, and I don't have a clear idea of what that might be," Anne shared.

"I'm sure God will lead you to your next step. He always has. You don't have the distractions that come with having a young family. I'm sure the quiet spaces are a little uncomfortable. But, hey, I can use some help decorating for the Women's Conference and help at the registration table, too," Karen said with a grin.

"You know I'll be there! You're absolutely right. God will show me how, where, and when to join in the work he has started. I just have to keep my eyes and ears open to opportunities," Anne said with determination.

"Wow, that pie was amazing! How about a little antiquing? We can multitask, walk off the calories we just enjoyed, and have fun shopping," Karen asked, still feeling a little guilty over having a slice of pie when she had been on Jeff about too many sweets.

"That sounds fantastic! Let me get the check, and we can head out."

It was a beautiful autumn day, the lingering warmth of summer mixed with slightly cooler breezes. The colors on the leaves had not yet turned. It was perfect weather for blue jeans and a sweatshirt. In a few short weeks, the trees that lined the streets would turn to brilliant shades of gold, red, and orange. Pumpkin lattes and hot apple cider would suddenly appear in every coffee shop and restaurant.

Karen and Anne shopped all afternoon, enjoying each other's company. Anne found a beautiful china teapot with four matching tea cups and saucers. They were the same pattern she remembered her grandmother had. Anne had been close to her grandmother. The two of them had tea parties often. Anne thought this was a great opportunity to continue the tea party tradition with her own granddaughters when they became old enough to enjoy a fancy tea party.

Karen found some fun items to add to the blessing bags she and the other women from church were putting together for the Women's Conference. They made a stop at the discount store for additional items to put in the bags.

Anne watched her friend shop and carefully select little things the ladies would be blessed with. She said a silent prayer, thanking Jesus for such a wonderful friend. Karen had been so understanding and had set aside two days for Anne even though she was in the midst of preparing for the conference. Anne felt truly blessed and deeply grateful.

Anne's phone rang. It was Tom.

"Sweetheart, Cade just called. He and Rachel are coming over in an hour, and they want to talk to us. Can you be home by then? I hate to cut your day short, but I know you wouldn't want to miss this chance to talk with them together," Tom said knowing she would be home right away.

"Of course, Tom. We were just finishing up anyway. I'll be home in half an hour. How's Mavis?"

Tom smiled and said, "Little Miss Mavis has had a pretty big day. She played with Great-Grandpa and Great-Grandma, rode the big tractor, helped feed the calves, had some ice cream at Justine's, and has been taking a nap for the past hour."

"That's fantastic! I'm so glad you two had a great day. I'll see you soon. Love you. Bye."

"Love you too, Anne."

Anne found Karen at the checkout counter ready to purchase the trinkets she thought were must-haves for the blessing bags.

"Karen, Tom just called, and I need to get home right away. Cade and Rachel are coming over in an hour to talk with us," Anne said, knowing her friend would understand.

"Perfect timing! I have everything I need. I'll just pay for these, and we can be on our way," Karen said, relieved that she had been successful in spending a fun day with Anne and getting all her errands run, too. Karen would start calling her volunteers as soon as she got home to begin coordinating their efforts.

The ladies made great time getting to Karen's house. They exchanged hugs, and Anne was on her way home. She prayed all the way there, asking God to be with Cade and Rachel and help them to be in the right mindset to begin to put their marriage back together. She also asked that the Lord be with the four of them as they discussed Cade and Rachel's relationship.

CHAPTER 17

Tom was on the porch swing with Mavis reading her favorite book, *The Poky Little Puppy*. She was not patient enough to let Tom read all the words on the page. Mavis took charge and turned the pages when she thought they should be turned. Both Mavis and Tom looked up when they saw Anne drive up the driveway. Mavis squirmed to get out of the swing as soon as she recognized Gamma was in the car.

"Well, there's my little Mavis! Were you good for Poppa?"

Mavis giggled, and Tom reached over to give Anne a quick kiss to welcome her home.

Tom suggested they go inside to talk. Mavis grabbed her book and her poppa's hand, and they went inside to the kitchen.

"Have you heard from Cade about how things have gone today?" Anne asked.

"No, other than his calling to tell me when they were coming to talk and pick up Mavis. He sounded exhausted. It had to have been a very difficult day for both of them. It also can't be easy for Rachel to come over with Cade to talk about everything with us. I credit you and your relationship with her for making her feel comfortable enough to talk with us."

"Tom, I'm really concerned. Rachel made a terrible mistake, and I don't know if Cade will be willing to forgive her and work to improve their marriage. I hate to see them break up. Mavis needs both her parents," Anne said with conviction.

Mavis sat happily on the floor with her wooden building blocks. When Cade and Rachel arrived, she was building towers, giving them a kick, and giggling as they tumbled over. Tom and Anne held their breath as Cade and then Rachel walked in. They both had dark circles under their eyes and looked haggard. Mavis spied her parents and went running toward them. Cade picked up his little girl as she nuzzled her tiny face in his neck.

Mavis broke the tension as she pulled her face away and said, "You scratchy, Daddy!"

Everyone laughed as Cade admitted he probably was scratchy since he hadn't shaved in a couple of days.

Mavis climbed back down and continued to play with her blocks. Tom motioned for everyone to have a seat around the kitchen table. Anne started pouring coffee for the four of them.

Rachel started the difficult conversation by saying, "We have had a pretty rough day, and it is all my fault. Cade has done nothing wrong, which is why what I did came as such a shock to him. If you are willing to listen, I would like to tell you both what happened. We shared all of this with Pastor Jeff today, and each time I share what happened, I am stunned by my level of self-deception and just how twisted my thinking became. I have been thanking God all day that I listened to your message, Anne. If I hadn't, who knows what would have happened."

Rachel then went into the details she had shared with Anne the night before. Cade stared at his shoes as Rachel talked about what she had done.

Cade slammed his fist on the table and shouted, "Enough! I can't hear this again. It might be cleansing to your soul, but it tears me apart. From everything you have said since you got home, there is nothing I can do to make things better. I trusted you, loved you, and supported you, and that wasn't enough. Rachel, you let another man into your life and destroyed all my trust in you, and you have destroyed our marriage. It's great that you came back so we don't have to worry that you're dead, but honestly, I don't know where we go from here. Our relationship will never be what it once was."

"Okay, emotions are high and you both must be exhausted," Tom intervened. Did Pastor Jeff give you suggestions for your next steps?" Tom hoped Jeff had given them clear direction.

"He suggested that, if possible, Mavis and I move back home for a couple of weeks until we can work through some of the hurt, disappointment, anger, and trust issues. Rachel will stay at our house and come to the farm to visit Mavis. She has agreed not to take Mavis back home until the three of us are ready to go back as a family. We are going to meet with Pastor Jeff two times a week to talk about how things are going. Will this arrangement work for you two? Ultimately, I do want us to be a family, but I'm not ready for that yet," Cade said earnestly.

Rachel tearfully said, "I don't blame Cade for wanting some time. It is going to be really hard not to have them home, but I understand. I am willing to do whatever it takes for as long as it takes."

Tom and Anne looked at each other and agreed to allow Cade and Mavis to move in with them for a few weeks, as long as they continued counseling with Pastor Jeff and working on their marriage. Cade went back home with Rachel to pick up some things that he and Mavis would need for the next two weeks. While Cade was gone, Anne got supper going, and Tom entertained Mavis.

Tom looked over toward Anne and said, "This is going to be a rough one. I know Rachel is genuinely sorry, but Cade is really hurt, and I'm not sure they can come back from this. If they do, it is going to take some time."

"I agree. I think the only thing we can do to help is provide a supportive, nurturing environment for them, and the rest is up to God to work in their hearts."

When Cade returned, Anne had a lettuce salad, stuffed chicken breasts, and corn on the cob ready for supper. Mavis was sitting in her high chair arranging and rearranging the Cheerios Tom had put on her tray. Cade came through the front door with a diaper bag and a suitcase.

"I'm beat. I have more things in the truck, but this is all we need for tonight. Thanks for letting us stay and helping me through this big mess. I can bring the rest of it in tomorrow morning," Cade said, truly exhausted.

He dropped off the diaper bag in the guest room, took his suitcase to his old room, and laid it on the bed. Cade looked around the room. Nothing had really changed since he had left. He thought to himself, *I never imagined I would be back sleeping in my room again.* Just then Tom joined his son.

"Cade, I want you to know that your mother and I love you and will do anything to help you through this. I am really proud of you for talking with Pastor Jeff today. I know that couldn't have been easy for you. Allowing your mother and I into your private business isn't easy either. Everything you have shared with us is confidential. If I know your mom at all, I can tell you that she is going to try to work with Rachel. She has continued to pray for the three of you since this whole thing started. We are solid, and you can rely on your family."

With that, Cade sat on the edge of his bed and cried. It had been years since he had shed a tear, but now he couldn't stop. He had no idea how his life could have gotten so messed up in such a short period of time. Now he had a child and a wife whose future teetered on the brink of destruction. He had no idea if he could or would be able to get over what Rachel had done and rebuild their marriage. Tom sat next to Cade and put his arm around his son's broad shoulders. He tried to comfort his son the best way he knew how: just being present for him.

CHAPTER 18

Over the next few days, Tom, Anne, Cade, and Mavis developed a schedule that worked for them. Anne continued to get up early to enjoy her quiet time with the Lord. Afterward, Tom spent time with Anne in the kitchen while she made breakfast for the family. Cade tended to Mavis and got her ready for the day. Each morning, Tom prayed before the meal, asking God's blessing on the food and that the Lord would do a mighty work in the hearts and minds of Cade and Rachel. Tom and Cade left for the farm after breakfast, and within an hour, Rachel was at the house ready to spend time with her precious daughter.

Cade and Clay worked together on the farm with Tom. Cade was grateful to have his little brother with him all day. Even though they often kidded each other, they had always been close and there for each other. They talked about the crisis Cade was going through, and each time, Clay assured his brother that he would support him whatever he decided to do with his marriage.

The phone rang, drawing Anne's attention away from watching Rachel and Mavis play. "Hey, Anne! I am in desperate need of your decorating expertise. I am looking at a pile of fabric, twinkling lights, flowers, and tulle. I have no idea what to do next. Can you meet me at the venue today and give me a hand?" Karen pleaded.

"Let me check with Tom and see if he had anything in mind for me to take care of today." Anne thought a minute and asked, "Do you mind if I bring Rachel along? I'm not sure if she is up to it, but it might do her good to be around some other positive women."

"I don't mind at all. The more, the merrier," Karen replied.

Rachel had been feeling a deepening sense of shame and guilt. Anne could sense Rachel starting to shut down and thought a little break from the heaviness of the situation might help her move forward.

Anne called Tom to make sure her day was truly open. He had nothing planned for her and agreed that it might be nice to get Rachel out with some other ladies.

"Rachel, how would you like to come with me to help Karen decorate the meeting room for the Women's Conference? You have great taste, and it would be fun doing something creative together. If you like, we can bring Mavis along, or I'm willing to bet that Great-Grandpa Stan and Great-Grandma Beth would be elated to spoil her for a couple of hours. What do you think?" Anne asked, hoping Rachel would consider the invitation.

"I don't know. I don't want to do anything that might upset Cade. I don't want him to think I'm trying to push Mavis off on his grandparents," Rachel replied, looking down at her feet.

"Whatever you decide is okay with me. Why don't you give Cade a call and let him know what I suggested and listen for his feedback? If he would rather you stay home with Mavis, I will honor that request. If you would rather not drop her off with Stan and Beth, you and Mavis could come along and give Karen and me some ideas about how to use the materials Karen has collected." Anne hoped Rachel would at least come along with Mavis.

Rachel called Cade, and he was comfortable with her taking the baby and riding along with Anne. Both Rachel and Cade agreed that it wasn't time to drop Mavis off at his grandparents' house. However, the conversation did lead to Cade suggesting that the three of them plan a visit to see his grandparents soon.

After the phone call, Rachel was grinning from ear to ear. That conversation helped her feel like there may be hope for their marriage. Cade thanked her for running the situation past him and asking for his input. It was actually the first time in their marriage that she had even thought to ask for and respect his opinion on something she was considering. Cade told her that it was a good first step in earning his trust. He also said he wanted to do something as a family again.

Rachel told Anne that she and Mavis would be happy to help decorate. Rachel got Mavis ready for the trip into town and buckled her car seat into the back seat of Anne's car. Rachel grabbed a bag full of Mavis's favorite toys and snacks. Both Anne and Rachel were excited to create a beautiful atmosphere for the women attending the conference.

Within an hour Anne, Rachel, and Mavis met Karen and a couple of other women from the church in the lobby of the Windsong Hotel. It became their mission to transform the formal conference room into an inviting atmosphere that would help the women attending the conference feel relaxed and comfortable. Karen had gathered items that would create a shabby chic environment. They decorated the registration table with old embroidered tablecloths and then placed bouquets of pink and white peonies in galvanized steel buckets on either end of the tables. Rachel took the stack of framed chalkboards and the pastel milk paint and created signs that would direct the women to different areas and activities during the conference. Anne placed a flowered tablecloth on a long table and arranged the blessing bags and folders containing the agenda for the event. Karen wrapped the twinkling white lights in the pale pink tulle and hung them up, creating a beautiful swag in the front of the room. At each end and in the middle of the swag, Karen attached a gorgeous arrangement of pink and white peonies. Mavis happily built block towers in her playpen.

After Rachel finished displaying her chalkboard signs, she picked up a folder and read through the Women's Conference agenda. Her eyes glanced over the topic for the keynote speaker on Friday night. Saturday morning, several breakout sessions were being offered on a variety of topics. Then her eyes settled on the topic scheduled for the speaker at 1:00 p.m. There in bold letters was the word *FORGIVENESS* and this description: "Learn about forgiveness of self and forgiveness of others." She felt her throat tighten and her heart race. This is one talk she knew she needed and the one talk she was terrified to attend. Rachel could feel an inner urging to attend the conference Saturday afternoon.

Anne looked up from her decorating and saw Rachel staring at a piece of paper with tears streaming down her face. Anne went to her and said, "Rachel, what's wrong? Are you okay?"

"I think I need to attend this talk. I feel like I need to hear what is going to be said for me to begin moving forward. I am so ashamed and haven't been able to forgive myself. I'm going to have to ask Cade if it will be all right for me to attend, if only for that one talk," Rachel said in an almost trancelike monotone.

"Rachel, if the Lord is calling you to attend the conference, he will make it possible for you to go. You simply have to ask him to clear the way. Then talk honestly to Cade about the conference and why you want to go. I will be at the conference, too. Karen has free babysitting available for the attendees. If Cade isn't comfortable with that, maybe he can take care of Mavis for the day or the afternoon so you can attend that talk," Anne suggested.

An hour later, Jeff arrived with the final touch for the Women's Conference. He used an old piece of barn board and pastel pinks and greens to paint a country welcome sign. It was the perfect finishing touch. Jeff and two of the maintenance men hung the sign above the front entrance.

With the decorating complete, Anne gave Karen a quick hug and promised to come an hour early to the conference to help with registration. Rachel collected Mavis and all her things and walked out to Anne's car. She put Mavis in her car seat and gave her some Goldfish and a sippy cup of apple juice—the obligatory car ride snack.

Rachel didn't say a word on the way back home. Anne could tell she was deep in thought, and rather than try to engage her in a conversation or pressure her, Anne simply offered to give her a ride to the conference if she chose to go. Rachel nodded, acknowledging the offer, but didn't speak.

As Rachel was unloading the car, Anne gave Tom a call.

"Tom, would it be okay if you and I went out for dinner tonight? I think the kids are going to need a little alone time. If we take off right away, it will give Cade and Rachel some time to talk without the two of us being there."

"Well, sure, I guess. Is everything all right?" Tom asked.

"I'm really hoping it will be."

"Okay, I'll let Cade know we are taking off right after I get home because I can't say no to his mother."

Anne laughed. "Thank you, honey. I'll try to remember how you can't say no to me the next time something super amazing comes up."

"We'll be home in an hour."

Rachel and Mavis were playing in the living room when Anne walked in. Rachel had put away all the toys and the diaper bag she used that day. Although Rachel looked somewhat distracted, she couldn't help but cherish her sweet daughter.

"Rachel, I just got off the phone with Tom. He and Cade will be home in an hour. Tom and I are going to take off right away for dinner. You two are welcome to the leftover fried chicken and coleslaw. Now that I think about it, there are four cobs of sweet corn on the back porch. If you want, you could boil them for supper, too."

Rachel's face brightened. She could see that Anne had created an opportunity for her and Cade to have time together to talk. Rachel could not believe how richly blessed she was. After all, how many mothers-in-law would have been willing to help save their son's marriage with everything that had happened?

Rachel walked out to the back porch and prayed, "Dear Lord, I am a wretched sinner, and I know I don't deserve anything. I believe you have called me to be at that conference this weekend. If it is your will for me to attend, please clear the way for me to go. I pray that Cade will be able to see that I truly want to pick up the pieces of my shattered life and marriage and put them back together again. It is all in your hands, Lord. Please give me the strength to have a good, honest conversation with Cade. Help him to be open to hear what I am asking for. I ask this in your sweet son Jesus's name. Amen."

While Anne was getting ready to go out for dinner with Tom, Rachel was busy preparing supper. Mavis was in her high chair pitching Cheerios over her tray and singing "Jesus Loves Me."

Soon after, Tom and Cade arrived. Rachel had taken care to set the table for the two of them. She carefully arranged each place setting on top of a fresh tablecloth. Tom came into the house, dropped off his lunch pail, and cleaned up. Then he and Anne were back in the pickup headed to Justine's.

Cade looked around and asked, "What's this all about? You have dinner for me, and Mom and Dad hightail it out of here."

"I think your parents thought it might be good for us to have a little time together without them. I didn't ask them to leave, if that's what you are wondering." Rachel immediately regretted her last statement. Why wouldn't Cade be suspicious after everything she'd put him through?

"I'm sorry, Cade. I didn't mean for that to come across snippy. It hasn't been that long, and you have no reason to trust me." Rachel looked down at the floor and sighed.

"Rachel, we have to stop walking on eggshells around each other. I know you are really trying. Let's start this evening over. Dinner smells great, the table looks nice, and it is good to sit down as a family; you, me, and Mavis," Cade said sincerely.

After dinner, they both gave Mavis her bath, got her ready for bed, and read her a story. After she was tucked in for the night, Cade built a fire in the firepit. He made some coffee and invited Rachel to join him. They sat together, gazing into the fire for a long time. Eventually, Rachel mustered up the courage to talk to Cade about the conference.

"Cade, there is something I'd like to ask you. I will honor your decision on this. I want us to be able to work through everything together," Rachel began.

"Okay, what is it?"

"Well, I simply can't forgive myself for the huge mess I have made of our marriage and our life together. It is entirely my fault, and I can't seem to move any closer to the future we can have together because of my shame. I need to somehow learn to accept my sin, take responsibility for it, and begin to see myself as a worthwhile person. While I was helping your mom and Karen decorate for the Women's Conference, I saw that the keynote speaker is going to give a talk on forgiveness Saturday at the beginning of the afternoon session. I wondered if you would be okay with my attending that talk. They provide free babysitting at the conference so I could take Mavis with me. Your mom offered to give me a ride to the conference and bring me back home afterward if I was going to stay for the day. I would really like, at the very least, to attend the talk on forgiveness, if that's okay with you. Please don't tell me it's okay with you unless you are truly comfortable with my going," Rachel said earnestly.

"I don't know, Rachel. Can I sleep on it?"

"Of course. I understand it is probably way too soon."

"I didn't say that. I would like to sleep on it and let you know in the morning," Cade responded gently.

Just then, Tom and Anne returned from their dinner out. They could see the slim silhouettes of Cade and Rachel against the fire. Cade gave Rachel a hug before she turned to go to her car and take the lonely ride back to their empty house.

"Hey, son! How was your evening?" Tom asked.

"It was a little weird. Rachel made me supper, and it started to feel like old times. She is really trying; it's just that I don't know if I can trust her again. She asked about attending that lady's thing you have going on this weekend, Mom. What do you know about it?" Cade asked.

"It's a Christian Women's Conference. Karen organizes it every other year. This year, she has some incredible speakers. I think it's going to help a lot of women grow closer to the Lord and help them work through some of the issues they may be facing," Anne shared.

"Rachel asked me if she could go to the conference. There is one talk in particular that she wants to attend. She said it's on forgiveness. That sounds like a talk I should listen to, not her," Cade said briskly.

"Honey, Rachel doesn't understand how she let sin into her life. Once Satan had a foothold, this mess took on a life of its own. She didn't guard herself, and Satan took her down a dark path that she is only beginning to pull out of. She hasn't been able to forgive herself, and without that, she has little hope that you or God will forgive her. Ultimately the decision is yours, but for what it's worth, I think she is being sincere. If she attends, she will be surrounded by our loving Lord and Christian women who can help her work through it. I know she was thinking about only going to the one talk, and if that is what you two decide is best, that's great. You should know that the talks prior to that prepare the ladies for the talk on forgiveness."

Tom added, "You know, Cade, it probably is a good idea that you learn more about forgiveness, too. Talk to Pastor Jeff about it. I'm sure he has a much better way to reach your heart than that ladies' meeting."

Cade smiled and said, "I know you're right, Dad. I will talk to Pastor Jeff about it. I think I will call Rachel and let her know she can go to the conference this weekend. I will drop her off and pick her up Friday and Saturday. I want us to have a little time together each day."

With that, Cade grabbed his phone and called Rachel.

The phone rang, and Rachel about jumped out of her skin. She looked and saw that it was Cade.

"Hello, Cade."

"Hi, Rachel. I thought about you going to the conference this weekend. I think it would be a good idea for you to go. I would like to drive you and Mavis there and home on Friday and Saturday. I know Mom offered to drive you, but I want us to have a little private time to talk. Is that okay with you?"

Rachel couldn't believe her ears. Cade not only wanted her to go to the conference but was willing to drive her and Mavis there and back. He actually wanted time with her alone. *God is good*, she thought.

"Well, is that okay, Rachel?"

"Um, well, yes! I'm so happy you are willing to drive us to and from the conference," Rachel said, relieved.

"Mavis and I will pick you up around 8:00 in the morning. That should be enough time to get you there, right?"

"That's perfect! Thank you, Cade!"

"Good night, Rachel."

"Good night."

CHAPTER 19

The rich aroma of the Jamaican brand of coffee wafted through the hotel lobby. The fresh bakery was perfectly arranged in lovely, cloth-lined baskets. Soft pastel tablecloths draped gently over the circular tables. A freshly poured carafe of coffee was placed in the center of each table with dainty coffee cups and saucers positioned in front of each chair. Karen had orchestrated a beautiful environment for the women to feel relaxed and cared for.

Anne found her spot behind the registration table. Karen walked around the corner and saw her best friend ready to welcome each guest and register them.

"I love you, Anne! You are the only person I know who is always where they promise to be, without exception."

"Of course I'm here. I think you might be a little tired and wound too tight this morning," Anne teased.

"Well, I'm dying to know. Is Rachel coming today?"

"As of last night, she is coming. Cade is going to drive Rachel and Mavis here. Do you mind praying for them before everyone gets here?" Anne asked.

Karen prayed, "Dear heavenly Father, I pray that Cade and Rachel learn to bear with each other and forgive each other as you, Lord, have forgiven them. Help them to be kind and compassionate to each other, forgiving each other just as Christ forgave us. This is a very difficult time for them. Please give them hope and the skills to reconcile their differences. Please do a great work in each of their hearts. I ask this in your precious son Jesus's name. Amen."

"Thank you, Karen. That was beautiful," Anne said sincerely.

Cade pulled up to the entrance of the hotel with Rachel and Mavis. After he parked the truck, Cade got Mavis out of her car seat and carried her into the lobby. Rachel came in behind them with the diaper bag and a new notebook for the day. They walked to the nursery, registered Mavis, and walked to the registration table where Anne sat ready to register Rachel.

"Good morning, you two!" Anne greeted them cheerfully.

Cade replied, "Morning, Mom. You don't need to bring Rachel and Mavis home. I'm going to come back at the end of the day to pick them up."

He then turned to Rachel and said, "I want you to have a good day. Text me when you are ready to be picked up. If you can give me a 30-minute heads-up, I can be here and you won't have to wait."

"I will do that. Thank you," Rachel said warmly as she squeezed Cade's hand.

With that, Cade got back in his pickup and headed to the farm. Rachel said a quick prayer, thanking God for Cade's willingness to work with her to repair their marriage.

Anne called over to Rachel, "Come on over here, Rachel. I'll get you registered and you can grab your folder, name tag, and a blessing bag and have a seat. I'm so glad it worked out for you to join us for the conference. You can run down to the nursery during breaks and lunch to check on Mavis."

By 9:00 a.m., everyone was registered and sitting in their seats. There was a buzz in the room. The much-anticipated keynote speaker had just arrived. Anne sat at a table for two at the back of the room. Karen would be taking the other seat after she welcomed the ladies and introduced Candice Spade, a very well-known Christian author and speaker. In fact, her latest book, *Living a Christ-Centered Life through Applying Scripture*, had become a bestseller. Candice generously donated a copy of the book to each woman in attendance.

Karen started the day off with a wonderful prayer, praising the heavenly Father and asking him to open the hearts and minds of the women in attendance so he could do a good work in them. Then Karen introduced Candice, who was welcomed with thunderous applause. When the ladies ended their applause, they were soon hanging on to every word Candice shared with them.

Anne scanned the room, looking for ladies in need of anything she might be able to help them with. So far, so good. Candice had all the women engaged in her talk. Anne saw Rachel sitting at a table with five other young married women, most of whom had children. Anne recognized them from church. She was glad to see that Rachel had joined a table with other women her age who would be facing some of the things young married women face. Soon Karen joined Anne, and the two of them sat back and began to enjoy the morning session.

By 11:30 a.m., Justine and her crew from the restaurant arrived and set up for lunch. She had prepared butternut squash and chicken and rice soup, turkey and roast beef sandwiches on croissants, and a fresh fruit and lettuce salad. For dessert, Justine had made pumpkin bars and frosted brownies. The lunch smelled amazing and tasted even better. It was a huge hit with the ladies. Rachel and two of the women from her table grabbed their lunches and took them to the nursery to eat with their children.

Although Anne was tempted to go to the nursery with Rachel to see Mavis, she held back. She was happy to see Rachel make some connections with the other ladies at her table and choose on her own to spend some time with Mavis. She did text Tom to let him know that things seemed to be going well for their daughter-in-law and granddaughter. Tom thanked her for the update because, honestly, it had been weighing heavily on his mind all morning. He knew it was tough for Cade to let Rachel go to the conference when they were barely hanging on as a couple.

The afternoon flew by with breakout sessions. They covered a variety of topics and were led by ladies from Karen's church and some surrounding area Christian women leaders.

Rachel texted Cade halfway through the last talk. She wanted to respect his wishes and was looking forward to seeing him as soon as the conference let out for the day. Rachel had actually begun to feel a little better as the talks continued throughout the day. She made a couple of new friends who also had small children. However, she wondered if they could possibly want to be her friend if they knew the truth about what had happened just a few short weeks ago.

At the conclusion of the day, Rachel picked up Mavis and tucked her folder, notebook, and book into Mavis's diaper bag. The two of them were waiting outside the hotel for Cade when he pulled up. Cade parked the truck and walked over to them. He picked up Mavis, grabbed the diaper bag from Rachel, and walked them back to the truck. Cade buckled Mavis into her car seat, closed the door, and then opened Rachel's door for her. That was a huge step forward for Cade.

"Well, how did it go today?" Cade asked.

"I was nervous at first, but the women there were all very nice. The speakers were good, and I took a lot of notes. I think the talks tomorrow will be more direct. It seemed like the speakers today were helping us get ready for the keynote speaker's talk tomorrow. I went to the nursery with some of the other moms and had lunch with Mavis. Thanks for asking," Rachel replied.

"I'll be honest, it was hard to let you go to the conference today. But Clay helped me realize that I have to start somewhere with trusting you, and this seemed to be a good beginning. Thank you for letting me know when you were going to be done for the day.

That text told me that you are taking me and us seriously. Rachel, I want my family back, but it is going to take some time for me to trust you again," Cade shared from his heart.

"I want our family back together, too, and you can take as much time as you need. I want to be the wife you deserve, which is a much-improved version of what I was before. Thank you for giving me and our marriage a chance."

Mavis was sound asleep in her car seat when Cade dropped off Rachel at their house. Rachel opened the door closest to Mavis and gently kissed her forehead before heading into the house. Then she thanked Cade for the talk and the ride home.

"I'll be over tomorrow morning at the same time, right?" Cade asked.

"That's right. I'll be ready and waiting, Cade."

Cade waved goodbye and drove to his parents' house. *Maybe there is hope for this marriage after all,* he thought to himself.

CHAPTER 20

The next morning, Karen and Anne arrived early to the conference just to make sure everything was ready for the ladies. The hotel staff did a great job cleaning and straightening up everything after the busy day before.

"Well, one day down, and today is looking pretty good," Karen said with a sense of relief. "This morning, we have the praise band coming to perform from 9:30 to 10:30, a breakout session, and lunch, and then Candice is going to give her talk on forgiveness at 1:00. That should take us to 2:30. From 2:30 to 3:30, she has agreed to do a question-and-answer session and end the day with a book signing."

"You have done an incredible job of promoting, organizing, decorating, and pulling this whole thing together, Karen. It is turning out to be an amazing event. Today is going to be fantastic. I noticed for today you just have a sign-in sheet for the ladies," Anne stated.

"Yes, registration really isn't necessary. Everyone who registered came yesterday. But I would like you to have the ladies sign in today because if anyone was unable to make it, I would like to touch base with them later to make sure they're okay."

"I'll make sure to have everyone sign in."

Just then Cade, Rachel, and Mavis arrived. They had made the same arrangements as the day before. This time, Cade and Rachel both seemed more relaxed. They walked down to the nursery together to drop off Mavis. Cade stopped by the registration table to greet his mom on his way out the door. Rachel signed in and made her way to the table she was seated at yesterday.

The ladies filed in and enjoyed a cup of coffee and fresh bakery treats while the praise band set up for the morning worship. The band started with a prayer and then sang "Closer" by Lifepoint. That song brought the whole group to a deeper place of praise and gratitude for the gifts of the heavenly Father. The band continued with other contemporary Christian praise songs.

Justine and her crew were back for day two and brought savory goodies for the ladies to enjoy. The soups, salads, sandwiches, and pie were arranged beautifully. Karen made sure there was enough for the hotel staff as well. She was so grateful to them for their wonderful service.

Karen had just received a note from Candice that she could not do her scheduled talk at 1:00 p.m. because she had lost her voice and could not speak. Candice felt terrible, but she couldn't get a word out. She did agree to stick around to sign books, but that was all she was going to be able to manage. Karen was praying for an answer to her dilemma when Anne came around the corner.

"Anne! I need your help! Candice has laryngitis and can't do her talk this afternoon. What are we going to do?" Karen implored.

"I don't know. Maybe Dawn Wills can fill in for Candice. She has led a number of women's groups. I bet she'd agree to do it," Anne suggested.

"She probably would if she were here. Dawn came yesterday and told me she couldn't make it today. Her goddaughter is getting married today." Karen sighed, not knowing what to do. Then it occurred to her. The one person who had plenty of experience forgiving others and herself was standing right in front of her!

"Anne, would you do it?" Karen asked.

"I'm not a speaker, and I have not led groups. You know me, I'm more of a behind-the-scenes kind of gal," Anne said rather matter-of-factly.

"Anne, please consider doing this. At least pray about it. I realize you prefer not to be the speaker, but you have had a lot of experience with forgiveness. I know you read Candice's book. Do you think you could come up with something for the 1:00 p.m. talk? I could help you put together an outline and be on a panel to answer questions."

"Let me have a few minutes to pray and think about it," Anne said.

Anne walked and talked to God. She felt a strong sense that she was supposed to help out Karen and the ladies by filling in for Candice. But with what? Anne continued to walk and pray and decided she would sketch out an outline and leave the rest to God. When she was finished with her outline, she shared it with Karen and said she would do her best to talk to the ladies about forgiveness. Then the two of them found Candice to have her go over Anne's notes.

Candice looked over Anne's notes and became teary-eyed. She grabbed another piece of paper and wrote, "That is perfect. God is using you today to help lots of women begin their process of forgiveness and grow closer to him. You are the perfect person to give this talk. I am going to stay in my room until you are finished. I don't want to be a distraction."

"You are going to sign your book for the ladies, aren't you?" Karen asked. Karen didn't think she could take another change in the schedule.

Candice took the paper and wrote, "Of course!"

Karen looked at her watch and saw that Anne had 15 minutes before the women would be filing back in to the conference room to hear Candice talk on forgiveness. Karen and Anne went into the conference room and shut the doors. They prayed together, asking the Holy Spirit to fill the room and do a wondrous work in the women attending the talk. They asked the Holy Spirit to fill Anne with the words he wanted her to share with the women. Just as they finished praying, there was a knock on the door.

Karen opened the door to allow the women back into the room. Once everyone was seated, Karen made the announcement that Candice would not be speaking. There was an audible groan. Then Karen explained, "Our very own Anne Williams has graciously agreed to give her talk on forgiveness. She has had a lifetime of working on forgiveness, both the forgiveness of others and herself. She will be sharing on a very personal level, and she is hoping each of you can open yourselves up to being honest with yourself and the Lord. Candice reviewed Anne's notes, and I can tell you that she was moved to tears. Candice will join us after Anne's talk to sign each of your books. Let's give Anne a huge round of applause and welcome her to the stage."

Rachel shifted uncomfortably in her seat. She thought about texting Cade to come and get her early. What was Anne going to share? *Is she going to share everything I put her and her family through?* Rachel thought about the new friendships she had formed and wondered how she would be judged. Rachel prayed and asked God to let her know if she should leave. She didn't get any kind of indication to leave or stay. She had clearly gotten a message from him about coming to the conference. God knew long before the conference was planned what was going to happen. Rachel reasoned that if she hadn't received a message from God to leave that she should stay put, no matter how uncomfortable she might feel. She had to trust that Jesus was going to continue to be there for her. If Anne brought up anything about her, she thought, she probably had it coming.

"Ladies, thank you for your understanding and willingness to welcome me to speak. I would not and could not be up here speaking to you without my Lord and Savior loving and supporting me through this. I am going to tell you that what I am going to share is personal to me. Let's pray."

Anne led the group in a prayer to help them move to a place where they would be willing to take an honest look at their own hearts. Rachel relaxed as she took in the prayer. She realized her fears were completely unfounded. Satan was trying to have his way with her again.

CHAPTER 21

Anne shared how the thread of forgiveness had been intricately woven into the fabric of her life. God's mercy was another colorful thread in that same fabric.

"Sometimes the lessons we learn about forgiveness and mercy come through direct experience, and other times they come through observation," Anne began. "As some of you know, my mother died of cancer when I was a teenager. Her illness was difficult for both my father and me. My mother spent hours with me so I could come to accept her illness and find the tender mercies our heavenly Father extolled on us. I remember feeling at times that it simply wasn't fair, but I never got to the point where I couldn't forgive God for what was happening to my family. My father, however, struggled deeply with the issue. He was angry that his family was being torn apart and his wife was going to be taken from him. I watched my mother with her God-given strength extend tender mercy to my father and forgive him for the things he had said and done in the height of strong emotions and depths of despair. She let us both know that Jesus was in the fight with us. I could cling to that knowledge and feel comfort. Not everyone can.

"Forgiveness is a multifaceted issue. Sometimes you are the person asking to be forgiven. Other times, someone else is asking you to forgive them. You may be angry with God and need to ask for forgiveness. Sometimes we wonder if we can even begin to forgive ourselves for mistakes or sins we have committed. I am not going to be able to give you one nice, neat answer wrapped up in a pretty bow for you to take home, but I can share with you a few thoughts to help get you on your personal path of forgiveness."

At this point in the talk, Candice slipped into the back of the room and sat with Karen at the table. Karen smiled at Candice and wondered why she chose to return early. Anne didn't seem to notice that Candice was in the room.

Anne continued, "I gave you an example of my being able to observe forgiveness and mercy with my parents during a very difficult time in my young life. This next example is a very tender spot in my heart. I had a very difficult time with postpartum depression following the birth of my second son. I had so much shame for not being able to care for my babies the first few months. I had to completely surrender to my husband and the Lord and let my family and friends jump in and take over. I felt stuck for the longest time. I had to come to the realization that postpartum depression is a real thing, and the debilitation that comes with it is nearly unbearable. It wasn't something I chose to have, and my inability to care for my boys or myself was completely out of character for me. The evil one had snuck in and fed me lies I began to believe. I thought I was a terrible mom and that my family would be better off without me. The vicious lies encircled and nearly consumed me. I had to let a Christian friend speak truth into me and pray with me. I asked both her and God for forgiveness, and it was granted to me. Slowly, I began to feel better, and my depression started to lift."

Karen heard a sniffle, looked over at Candice, and saw that she was weeping. Karen put her arm around Candice and comforted her as Anne continued.

"As you can see, I am pulling from personal experiences because I know them best, and the Lord is directing this talk. Another example happened when my oldest son was in high school. One of his teachers was bullying him. It went on for a long time before we were made aware of the situation. The mama bear in me wanted to, well, let's just say I didn't have a Christian thought about her at that time. I also felt just terrible that my son had been subjected to her nastiness for way too long. It took a huge effort on the part of my son, his friends, and their families to make the school board aware of the teacher's behavior. The hand of God was present at that school board meeting. When the details and a recording of her behavior were being exposed, I was asked to step out of the meeting with the other students. I felt the Lord moving me to pray for that teacher and forgive her publicly with the students. After praying for her and forgiving her, I felt a huge sense of relief and peace.

"Forgiveness of others is truly more for you than for them. Refusing to forgive others, or yourself, really keeps you imprisoned. By that I mean thoughts of the wrongdoing will continually haunt you, and it will be impossible to let it go and move forward. Jesus died on the cross for our sins. If he can forgive all us wretched sinners, who are we to not forgive?

"There is so much wisdom in the women in this room. I think we should break into smaller groups where we can discuss with each other the type of forgiveness we are struggling with and pray together. Let's have the women who would like to discuss self-forgiveness move to the table on my right. The ladies who would like to discuss the process of forgiving others can sit at the table directly in front of me. The ladies who would like to talk about asking God for forgiveness, move to the table to my left. Karen and I will join each table for a few minutes. Ladies, remember that what is said during these discussions stays in this room. This is a very emotionally laden topic, and for each of you to truly work on forgiveness, you need to feel free to open up and be honest with your sisters in Christ. You can go ahead and move to the tables."

The ladies responded to Anne's inspirational talk and transparency with a huge round of applause. Several had tears in their eyes and hugged their friends before they moved to the tables for the discussion they felt led to participate in.

Just then Anne saw that Candice was in the room and moving to the table where they were discussing self-forgiveness. Anne grabbed Karen and asked, "How long has Candice been in the room?"

"She came in just after you got started. I was just as surprised as you. She told me that she had a nudge from God to come in and listen to your talk. I think it had a pretty profound effect on her."

"If it did, it was God speaking through me to reach Candice. Oh look, the ladies are really getting into their discussions. Maybe we should join them," Anne suggested.

Anne purposefully chose a table where Rachel was not seated. She hoped that by keeping her distance, Rachel would feel comfortable enough to open up to the other women.

As Anne sat down, she tuned in to one particular woman, Jennifer, who shared that she thought God had been ignoring her and her family. "Friends have told me that everything happens for a reason. There was no good reason for God to take Aaron away, and nothing good has come of his death," Jennifer said emphatically.

Jennifer's husband, Aaron, had died of brain cancer two years ago. Prior to his illness, he and Jennifer had a great life. They had two daughters, ages six and four. Jennifer knew that she and the girls were the center of Aaron's universe. Without him leading and loving the family, Jennifer felt lost. She admitted to spending the last two years angry with God, blaming him for destroying her family and her future.

Anne asked Jennifer, "What made you decide to come to the conference?"

"My friend Angie suggested it. She said we could have a great girl's weekend, and this conference would just be a little part of it. I guess Angie knows me pretty well and knew exactly what I needed," Jennifer said as she smiled at her friend.

"Jennifer, how are you feeling now?" another woman asked.

"Well, I'm not really angry anymore. I'd say I'm feeling more confused than anything. Why did God take my Aaron just as we were starting our lives together? Why did he take my daughters' father away from them?"

"Honestly, those are great questions," Anne replied. "Now bear with me a minute. I hope this doesn't come across too strong. Have you thanked God for the time you had with Aaron? Or have you thanked him for experiencing the immense joy of being Aaron's wife and the mother of his children? Have you ever thought that maybe the time you had with Aaron was a sacred gift from God? Obviously, you loved him deeply, and together the two of you, with God's divine intervention, created two beautiful daughters. Certainly, you and the girls are going to miss Aaron, and he will always have a piece of your heart, but maybe God in his ultimate wisdom gave you, Aaron, and your daughters exactly what all of you needed."

Jennifer began to tear up and said, "I never thought about it that way. God did give me a tremendous gift by putting Aaron in my life, even if it was for a short time. I need to ask for forgiveness and tell God just how grateful I am."

Angie and the other ladies at the table were stunned. They had been so focused on Jennifer's sorrow that it had not occurred to any of them that there was anything in that situation to praise God for. Other women began to share how they had blamed God for difficult or painful situations and had failed to look deeper to find something to be grateful for or praise God for.

Once the conversations began to slow down, Jennifer asked if they would all pray together for a grateful heart. The women held hands, and each one said a prayer. After the prayer was over, Anne recited James 1:2–4:

> *Consider it pure joy, my brothers and sisters, whenever you face trials of many kinds, because you know that the testing of your faith produces perseverance. Let perseverance finish its work so that you may be mature and complete, not lacking anything.*

Karen and Anne swapped tables. The ladies at Anne's table continued talking about how they were going to go forward with their newfound insights. Karen picked up right where Anne left off. She offered words of encouragement and practical application of the forgiveness tools they'd just learned.

Anne found that at the next table, the women were into a deep conversation about people from their past whom they simply couldn't find in their hearts to forgive. Anne asked if they would stop for a moment and pray. She was well aware that this topic was one that she needed to rely on Jesus to work in everyone's heart for healing to take place.

Anne prayed, "Dear heavenly Father, we have all been hurt at one time or another by another person, whether intentional or not. Sometimes the hurtful incident is minor; other times, it is heinous. Create in each of us a forgiving heart. We are not saying that what happened to us was okay, but rather we need to forgive as you have forgiven. Teach us, Lord, to open the doors of our self-imposed prisons of anger, bitterness, and resentfulness. Let us move on from being a victim to becoming a person who can thrive with your loving grace and tender mercies. Your love is greater than any of us can comprehend, just as your forgiveness is hard for us to comprehend. Lord, we ask in the words of Paul in Ephesians 4:31–32 to help us *'Get rid of all bitterness, rage and anger, brawling and slander, along with every form of malice. Be kind and compassionate to one another, forgiving each other, just as in Christ God forgave you.'* We ask this in your precious son Jesus's name. Amen."

Maggie was the first woman to speak after the prayer. She said, "I can't remember the last time I wasn't filled with bitterness. It seems like everything I think about and experience is through the lens and heart of a woman whose husband left her for another woman. What's so sad is that my husband left me 20 years ago. I have allowed his desertion to fester into an ugly all-consuming monster in my life. The idea of breaking out of my self-imposed prison is exciting, but I don't want to let him off the hook."

Anne asked, "Who has been on the hook for the past 20 years? Him or you?"

Maggie swallowed hard and said, "It's been me on the hook, and I put myself there. Oh, my goodness. I can't believe I never saw it that way before."

"That is how Satan worms his way into our lives," Anne added. "He catches us in a vulnerable state, and once he finds our weakness, he jumps all over it. That is why we need to rely on our heavenly Father and his Word. Having sisters in Christ is helpful, too. Having good Christian friends who can reflect back to us what they see in our lives in a loving way helps us make corrections. The most important relationship, above all, is our relationship with Jesus Christ. That is where we find the comfort and the healing we all need."

Karen gave Anne the signal that it was time to switch to the last table. After the group discussions, Candice was going to sign copies of her book. Karen wanted to make sure that Candice signed a book for every lady in attendance. Anne didn't want to go to the last table on self-forgiveness. There sat her beautiful daughter-in-law who had very nearly destroyed her marriage with her son. Anne recognized that she needed to forgive Rachel or she would be a hypocrite. She couldn't give a talk on forgiveness and not forgive her daughter-in-law.

Anne ducked into the hallway for a quick prayer. She asked the Lord to help her forgive Rachel and be open to whatever she chose to share at the table. Anne walked toward the table, knowing what she needed to do to be obedient to her Lord.

Anne joined the table just as Rachel started to share her struggle with self-forgiveness. She opened up to the women and told them that she had left her husband and daughter to run off with another man. Anne sat at the table with tears streaming down her face. Rachel shared with the ladies that her shame had been so deep that she had been considering suicide. She hadn't been able to ask for forgiveness because she couldn't forgive herself.

Just then Natalie, Rachel's newfound friend, spoke up. "Rachel, you are a daughter of the most high King. You stumbled and fell. Your knees are scraped up, and your pride is hurt. Ask your heavenly Father to forgive you. He is aching to pick you up and hold you in his tender, loving arms. He knows you and everything that happened, and he is standing here waiting to accept you back into his flock. He doesn't want to lose any of his children."

Rachel sobbed. Natalie put her arm around her and urged her, "Honey, just ask, and you will be forgiven."

Anne put her hand on Rachel's hand and through her tears said, "Rachel, I forgive you."

After hearing the very familiar voice of her mother-in-law, Rachel looked up and said to Anne, "Thank you."

Rachel then got on her knees and prayed to God for forgiveness. When she sat back down, Rachel told the group that she felt as though a huge weight had been lifted and that she was ready to move on with her life with Jesus. She said, "With Jesus, I know I can face anything. I hope my marriage can be saved and that my husband can forgive me. His forgiveness of me is between him and

God, and I can't control that. I can, however, love him and our daughter with all my heart. I can promise him that I will protect my heart. Oh, and by the way, ladies, this amazing woman who just told me that she forgives me is my mother-in-law."

The ladies at that table were witnesses to God's amazing healing in the hearts of broken, hurting women. They saw that healing and forgiveness come from honestly pouring out your heart to the Lord.

Candice had remained at that table the entire time. She was blown away by the level of honesty and openness as the women shared. She decided to take a risk and share with them as well. She then disclosed to the group that she had not actually written the book she had given them. She said the true author never wanted her identity revealed. When the real author's books began to sell, she needed someone to represent her. Candice worked for the publishing company when her employer proposed the idea that she step into the role of the actual author. Candice thought, *Why not? It certainly can't hurt anyone, and it is easy money.* So she stepped into the role doing book signings and guest appearances to promote the book.

"Well, one thing led to another," Candice said, "and suddenly I found that I was beginning to believe the publicity about myself— uh, I mean the actual writer. I am so sorry. I just can't go on living this lie. I can't in good conscience sign books that I did not write. I think God had his hand in my losing my voice and then restoring it just enough to talk to you after I was brought face-to-face with the truth. I hope you can forgive me. I cannot disclose the true author of this book, but I can tell you that it isn't me."

The women ended the session in prayer, each one giving hugs and encouragement to one another. Candice had found a group of loving, forgiving Christian women she wanted to emulate. She retreated to her hotel room and phoned the author to let her know what had happened. She let the author know that she would no longer be representing the book or doing speaking engagements.

She was done acting and wanted to become the person God had intended her to be.

Karen gathered all the women together for a closing prayer. She was sending them home with a set of forgiveness skills and new Christian friends to help them traverse the bumpy road of a Christian woman.

Both Karen and Anne were exhausted. They sat alone at the registration table reviewing the past two days. Some ladies were blessed beyond measure. Others had just started their walk with Christ, and others learned the importance of listening to God's still, small voice and acting on it. A few women were about to start the process of forgiveness. A few others came to know Jesus as their Lord and Savior. It was an overwhelming success.

Out of the corner of her eye, Anne saw Rachel walking to the lobby with Mavis in tow. Cade walked into the lobby to greet them. Rachel handed Mavis to Cade and asked if he could wait with the baby for a couple of minutes.

Then Rachel walked over to Anne and gave her a big hug. "You have given me a tremendous gift. If you hadn't been able to forgive me, I don't know if I could have asked God for forgiveness. Thank you, thank you, thank you!" Then Rachel turned toward her husband, determined with the help of Jesus to repair their relationship.

Chapter 22

"Well, my friend," said Anne, "I'm beat, and it's time for me to go home. I'm sure Jeff is looking forward to having you back home, too. Tom texted a while ago and said he is picking up takeout for supper tonight. I love that man. He knows exactly what I need when I need it." Anne was ready to get home and enjoy a quiet night.

"I wonder if the guys talked," added Karen. "Jeff sent me a text saying he was going to pick up dinner for the two of us. We do have a couple of keepers!"

Karen did a quick scan of the room and saw that everything that needed to go back with her was already in the van. Anne looked around to see if anyone had accidentally left anything behind, but she found nothing. They shut off the lights and walked to their cars, both thankful for a transforming conference.

Tom had a crackling fire going in the fireplace in the den. He set the carryout boxes on the coffee table along with a bottle of Anne's favorite wine and two wine glasses. Anne walked up the front steps of her house and was greeted by her husband with a big hug and a welcome home kiss. She slipped off her jacket and shoes and followed him into the den. They enjoyed the crackling fire as they ate dinner and finished the wine.

"I don't know what happened at that lady's conference this weekend, but I can sure sense a change in Cade," Tom shared. "He said

Rachel has been trying really hard. She has been asking for his opinion and respecting his wishes."

"It is probably too early to tell for certain," Anne added, "but I do think they are on the right path. They just need to rely on God and keep him at the center of their marriage."

"Rachel's willingness to allow Cade to lead, treating him with respect and honoring his requests, has gone a long way with him. I know it won't be easy, but he is beginning to soften. He really loves Rachel and Mavis," Tom said, very proud of the family man his son had become.

"I know he does. And Rachel wants to change and truly wants him back in her life. I just realized something," Anne remarked.

"What's that?"

"We are sitting here alone. Cade didn't come back with Mavis for the night," Anne said, surprised.

Tom smiled. "I wondered how long it would take for you to notice. Cade came home at noon and grabbed most of Mavis's things and his own in hopes that the three of them would start spending the night together at their house."

"Wow! That's terrific! I hope they are both ready for it."

"Don't worry. Cade didn't spring it on her. They talked during one of the morning breaks and decided to give it a try."

Tom reached for Anne's feet and gently gave her a foot massage. Anne threw the quilt over both of them and snuggled into the couch, allowing herself to sink into the sofa and finally relax. She was completely content with the man she loved and a heavenly Father who holds her in his hand.

The next morning over coffee, Tom asked, "Anne, how are you doing, really?"

"Well, I feel a lot more like myself after that amazing foot rub last night. I'm sorry I fell asleep so early. I guess I was really exhausted. I never would have thought the weekend would wipe me out like that," Anne said, a little embarrassed that she wasn't able to keep her eyes open once Tom started to rub her tired, aching feet.

"That isn't what I was referring to. You had been really down, not knowing what your purpose is and questioning what kind of kingdom work you had been involved with. How is that going? You seem more like yourself again, but I would like to know what has been going on in that head of yours."

"Oh, that," Anne said coyly. "Well, I am beginning to feel much better. In fact, I think I am starting to pull together some ideas how I can better serve the Lord going forward. I want to talk to Karen more about it and flesh it out a little further. But to better answer you, I don't feel panicked about my role in life or turning 50 anymore. Thank you for always being there for me, no matter what is going on in my life. Actually, you are an amazing husband, father, and grandpa. I love you!"

With that, Tom and Anne went upstairs to get ready for church. Once they were both ready, Tom grabbed the truck keys, and he and Anne drove off to church. On the way there, Tom said a silent prayer, thanking God for the sweet, humble, loving wife he had the privilege to share life with.

That afternoon, Anne called Karen to set up a coffee date. "Happy Sunday afternoon," Anne said, full of cheer.

"Um, happy Sunday to you. I know Jeff gave a great sermon, but I didn't expect you to be this inspired," Karen said, knowing from Anne's tone that something had truly changed for her. She was positive and full of the energy she had possessed prior to that darn invitation to AARP.

"Listen, I really want to talk to you about something I am super excited about," added Anne. Tom and I are going to spend the rest of the day together, but I'm hoping you're up for a coffee date first thing tomorrow morning. The coffee and treats are on me."

"Sure. I'm going to catch up on some rest today, but I'll be ready for you to pick me up at 8:00 a.m. tomorrow," Karen said. Karen could tell that something important had changed for Anne. She would have liked to push back the time to 10:00 a.m. but knew Anne would be there by 8:00 a.m. anyway.

Anne was right on time the next morning. Karen jumped into Anne's car, and the two of them were soon on their way to Perk Place for the promised cup of coffee.

"Well, what's up?" Karen asked.

"Not until I get a cup of coffee in you," Anne teased.

"I'm good with that. It's better to wait. We both know that I think better after a hot cup of steaming wake-up juice."

Soon the two friends were seated in a booth with fresh coffee and warm blueberry muffins. Karen took a sip of her coffee and said, "Okay, I am in a good spot to have a deep conversation. Thanks for pulling this all together. You have always paid attention to the little things that make everyone feel loved and important."

"You are too kind. You have done a great job of reminding me of some big events in my life, and then the Lord chose to use me to glorify him and advance his kingdom. Thank you so much for that. This weekend helped me have a sense of what I might be able to do to continue in kingdom work."

"Are you thinking of speaking at women's conferences, Anne? I think you would be phenomenal. You did such a great job over the weekend. I can see you influencing lots of women through that type of work."

"Not exactly. You, my friend, taught me a lot about day-to-day excellence that women are charged to do as part of our kingdom work. Sure, the big things happen occasionally and we need to be prepared for those times. But I think it is the day-to-day things that women do that seldom get noticed but make a huge accumulating effect on the lives of their husbands, families, and friends. I think women of all ages need to know that doing everything they do, whether it is greeting newcomers at church, serving a cup of coffee, or scrubbing toilets, is noticed and important to our heavenly Father. I want to be able to share that message with women of all ages. I don't know exactly what that is going to look like. Think about it. It is one of the many messages my mom gave to both of us. I think it had a profound influence on us. What if we could share that message with many women? What if we could get ladies to meet together and hold one another accountable and encourage and edify one another?" Anne continued to share her God-given vision with Karen.

Karen and Anne tossed ideas back and forth all day. They prayed and invited the Lord into their conversation and plans.

CHAPTER 23

Anne responded and obeyed the direction of her heavenly Father. She spent anywhere from a few minutes to a few hours each day praying for guidance, researching the Bible, discussing ideas with other women, and putting her thoughts on paper.

Within six months, Anne had written her first book. She shared it with her best friend, Karen, made some changes, and prayed over it. When Anne and Karen were reasonably sure the book was ready for publishing, they contacted their friend in publishing Candice Spade. She had returned to her former role at the publishing company and now personally handed Anne's manuscript to the decision maker.

Six months later, Anne's book was in print and on bookstore shelves. It became a bestseller and remained on the bestseller list for 12 weeks straight. The overwhelming success of the book was no surprise to Karen or Tom, but Anne was stunned. The publisher asked Anne to develop a workbook and study guide to accompany the book.

Anne prayed, asking the Lord for guidance regarding a study guide. After getting the sense from him that she should go ahead with the project, she started working on it. When Anne completed the study guide, she insisted on doing a trial run with some women at church before submitting it to her publisher. She wanted to make sure it made sense and that the women found it useful.

The women loved the book and the study guide. Anne made a couple of minor changes and submitted it to her publisher. Within a few short months, it was in print and widely circulated.

Just as Anne was starting to feel like things were slowing down and this project the Lord had laid on her heart was complete, she got an unexpected call.

"Anne Williams?" the unfamiliar woman on the other end of the line asked.

"Yes, this is Anne."

"This is Judy Jameson from Women's Life Christian Conferences in Atlanta, Georgia."

"Hello, Judy. I am familiar with your organization. In fact, I have attended several of your conferences. What can I do for you?" Anne asked.

"Anne, I would like to schedule a time to meet with you to talk about possibly joining our group of speakers. Your message about forgiveness is transforming women's lives. You could spread your message further and faster by speaking at our conferences," Judy explained.

"You are very kind, but I am not a professional speaker. Are you sure you want me?" Anne asked, both overwhelmed and a bit confused.

"Let me ask you, Anne. Are you open to meeting for a conversation with me? We can go over the details, and you can decide after you have all the information."

"Okay. My husband and I can meet with you on Monday morning. Can you meet with us here at our home?" Anne asked.

"Of course. I would love to meet at your home. How's Monday at 10:00 a.m.?"

"That will work. If you give me your email address, I will send you directions to our house."

The meeting with Tom, Anne, and Judy went well. After much discussion and prayer, Anne connected again with Judy and agreed to join the speaking staff of Women's Life Christian Conferences. The organization provided training for Anne to help her feel more confident speaking to large groups of women. Anne agreed to speak six times per year for Women's Life Christian Conferences.

As the new season of conferences began, Karen diligently straightened the display of Anne's books and study guides. When Anne joined Women's Life Christian Conferences, Karen volunteered to help by organizing and running Anne's booth at the various conferences. Anne discovered that she had the gift of speaking directly to a woman's heart. Karen loved having a supportive role in Anne's new endeavor. Rachel, who had given birth to Ruth, the couple's second little girl, now joined Anne and Karen on the speaking tour. Rachel not only introduced Anne but gave an impressive talk on forgiveness and marriage.

The lights dimmed in the auditorium, and a hush came over the room. "Ladies, I'd like to introduce our keynote speaker for today. She is the woman who has taught us all to take our kingdom work seriously and has helped us know that what we do, no matter how great or small, must be done with excellence to glorify our heavenly Father. She is my mentor and my mother-in-law. Please welcome to the stage Anne Williams."

"Welcome, daughters of the most high King!"

Afterword

My heavenly Father is the one who placed this book on my heart to write. The process of writing *A Daughter of the Most High King* was unlike any other writing experience I have ever had. I believe it is important that you, the reader, know what happened in the writing process once I became obedient to the task that was placed on my heart.

I am typically a very detailed, organized person. When given a writing assignment in college, I would usually engage in extensive research, write copious notes, and then prepare a detailed outline that would serve as a structure for my writing.

With this book, I tried to employ my usual method of writing, but it didn't go anywhere. So I didn't write an outline or do research of any kind. Instead, I relied on the Holy Spirit through prayer to formulate the concepts for this book. I committed to the Lord that I would write something every day until his book was complete. I couldn't wait to have the opportunity to sit at my computer each day and become inspired. Truly, I did not know from one day to the next what twist or turn this story would take.

I am so grateful to have worked so intimately with my Lord and Savior. It is my prayer for you, my dear reader, that when you know the Lord is asking you to do something for him, you will obey him immediately. And it is my prayer that you will be changed and blessed forever by the experience.

—Kim

www.ingramcontent.com/pod-product-compliance
Lightning Source LLC
Chambersburg PA
CBHW030839090426
42737CB00009B/1035